RICHMOND AWAKENING

City of Slavery. City of War. City of Freedom.

"If the Son sets you free, you will be free indeed."

BY DOUGLAS MCMURRY

©2005 by Douglas McMurry
Published by Bethlehem Books
2557 Hickory Knoll lane
Richmond, VA 23230

Printed in the United States of America

Unless otherwise noted, all scripture quotations are taken from the
New International Version of the Bible, copyright 1973, 1978,
1984 and 1995 by Zondervan Corporation.

ISBN 0-914869-01-9

ACKNOWLEDGMENTS

I wish to thank the many people who helped me evaluate and edit this manuscript: Andrew Fuller, Walter Varvel, Don Coleman, Eric Samuelson, William Carter, and Matthew and Sherrie Moore. I also wish to thank the people at the International House of Prayer in Kansas City, where God pumped vision into my life, much of which is expressed in this volume. Let me give special thanks for proofreading to Bill York and my daughter Elizabeth, and for typesetting and cover design to John Lindner and Page Hayes. Thanks to my friends of the Timothy Project for their support, and for their faithfulness to the vision of the Kingdom of God at Richmond.

ACKNOWLEDGMENTS

PREFACE

Twenty years ago, God brought my wife, Carla, my four children, and me to Richmond from the West coast. This happened through specific divine guidance having to do with "watering a church another man has planted."

However, I knew in my heart that there was another reason God wanted me in Richmond: to shoulder a burden to pray for Richmond, the capital of the Confederacy. I knew that I would eventually shed my local-church ministry and take on a city-wide ministry grounded in much prayer. Several people, including a few of my most trusted elders, confirmed this calling for me through the nineteen years I was pastor at Christ Presbyterian Church.

After leaving my pastoral charge in March of 2004 to take up this city-wide ministry of prayer, I was involved in an intense (at least, I thought it was intense!) season of fasting and prayer. I did this according to God's instruction, to find a clearer definition of what He wanted for and from me following 35 years as a local church pastor. During that time in August of 2004, while at the

International House of Prayer in Kansas City, God gave me a picture of what He wants to do here in Richmond in the future. I believe He gave me a message of hope and redemption for Richmond. The purpose of this book is to present that message in light of Richmond's unique history.

Richmond Awakening is the second book in a series I have written for Richmonders. The first was *The Church at Richmond*, published in 2003. I write this second book in the certainty that God wants to use the Church of Richmond in His plans for Richmond. The Church, after all, is equipped with the inheritance of Christ, an incomparable treasure of power, hope and love flowing from God's throne of grace. If we could be better connected to that throne of grace, how great a blessing we would be to our city!

Douglas McMurry
dougmcmurry@wholecity.net

CONTENTS

PART FOUR: HOW DO WE REALLY FEEL ABOUT THE POWER OF GOD?

Part One

JESUS
THE MIGHTY WARRIOR

Chapter One

A SURPRISING WORK OF GOD

In October, 1998, God accomplished a quiet miracle in Richmond. He began to call an entire continent to prayer. That prayer movement has emerged into a massive global prayer movement that has brought astonishing results.

A Visitor from Cape Town

While the Rev. Trevor Pearce of Cape Town, South Africa, was visiting Richmond, he happened to hear an audio-taped address by George Otis, Jr., describing how God had swept Cali, Colombia free of its drug cartels. This prayer-caused turnaround in a city known for its drug trafficking fired faith and hope in pastor Pearce. He returned to Cape Town determined to spread the word.

The following year, he happened to be in Washington D.C. at the very time George Otis, Jr. was introducing his *Transformations* video, which tells the story of Cali. He stocked up on the new videos and returned to South Africa prepared to distribute hundreds of them to church and city leaders. (To date, over 20,000 videos have been distributed to African leaders desperate for hope to see God move with power on their continent.)

Soon, Cape Town pastors were leading stadium-size prayer meetings every three months, eager to see a similar transformation in their city. These meetings reflected a Christian unity and fervency unseen in Cape Town since the city's beginnings. What happened next is described by leaders of a prayer movement now known as Transformation Africa:

> *The very mention of the illegal makeshift structure attached to a council house in the center of Manenberg, known as "Die Hok" (The Cage) would strike fear into the hearts of all those who knew it. This den of iniquity belonged to Rashied Staggie and the Hard Livings Gang. However, when Rashied was converted during 1998-1999, one of the first things that he did was to release this den of iniquity, and walked away from it by handing it over to the church. Die Hok is now a wonderful example of God's transforming power and its influence is felt all over Manenberg.*

It was Pastor Henry Wood who took up the challenge to plant a church in Die Hok. Some rudimentary changes were made to this former discotheque, bar, drug dealing hideout and venue of gunfights and death. It was with great relief that locals began to recognize with thankfulness this act of God and several began to make this venue their place of worship. Die Hok has since become a beacon of hope to this very needy community. Manenberg is known as the drug-dealing centre of Cape Town. Unemployment rates are in excess of 40%. It was also home to a number of rival gangs. The social circumstances were a recipe for disaster, with an average of three murders taking place each week—besides the gang fights, assaults, rape, robbery, etc.

Things began to change as Pastor Henry Wood began to preach the gospel of Jesus Christ, lead prayer walks through Manenberg and began to address the many social needs.... A centre for social empowerment by day and a church by night, the influence of this once notorious venue is felt all over Manenberg. The church has grown so large that it had to move to another venue in a public facility. The practical work of social transformation continues to be led from Die Hok...

The impact on the community is such that Pastor Wood recalled a period of 6 months during which there were no gang fights and no murders.[1]

An Explosion of Prayer

The clear demonstration of God's power in answer to massive Christian prayer encouraged the spread of the prayer movement to other cities and countries. Soon other leaders emerged to carry the vision to another level.

Graham Power, a board member of Western Province Rugby, received a vision from God for stadium prayer events throughout all of Africa. By 2002, he was organizing prayer meetings in dozens of cities, asking God for a continent-wide spiritual awakening based on 2 Chron. 7:14: "If my people, who are called by my name, will humble themselves and pray and seek my face and turn from their wicked ways, then will I hear from heaven, and will forgive their sin and heal their land."

The growth of this movement has been exponential, like dry twigs catching fire. By 2003, 360 cities and towns in South Africa, and 62 key cities in other countries were caught up in the movement. What began in Cali had spread, via Richmond, to the entire continent of Africa. Today, these efforts have morphed into a Global Day of Prayer each Pentecost.

Why Not Richmond?

By now it is clear: there are reproducible principles which, if the Christian Church followed them, we would find that God is ready to pour out His blessings here in Richmond, as in Cape Town and Cali. These principles grow out of prayer. They are rooted and grounded in Christian prayer, gaining access to God through the shed blood of Jesus. These hopes are rooted in the New Covenant:

> *I pray also that the eyes of your heart may be enlightened in order that you may know the hope to which he has called you, the riches of his glorious inheritance in the saints, and his incomparably great power for us who believe. That power is like the working of his mighty strength, which he exerted in Christ when he raised him from the dead and seated him at his right hand in the heavenly realms, far above all rule and authority, power and dominion, and every title that can be given, not only in the present age but also in the one to come. And God placed all things under his feet and appointed him to be head over everything for the church, which is his body, the fullness of him who fills everything in every way. (Eph. 1:18-23)*

This passage makes the Church the greatest asset of any city, the conduit for the power of God pouring into that city to bless it with His love. This power, however, must meet with faith and prayer, which draw the presence and power of God into a city. God wants His Church to be a house of prayer, a fiery furnace of love and faith which results in the manifestation of God's power to bless lost and desperate people, to liberate captives, to comfort those who mourn, and to teach us all over again how to love one another.

God can do such things in cities. He has done them before in our country's history, and He can do them again. He is doing these things in other countries, and I believe (and articulate in the pages below) He will do them again in our country—and in Richmond. But the Church needs to attune itself to these promises or, like the Sanhedrin in first-century Jerusalem, we will fail to interpret the signs of the times, and miss our golden opportunity. Spiritual blindness could actually cause us to oppose the work of God because we have inadvertently wandered far from Him without realizing it.

The obvious question for us in Richmond is: if Richmond became the gateway for a powerful move of God in Cape Town spreading into all of Africa, why hasn't Richmond become the gateway for a similar move of God *in Richmond*?

This is a serious question deserving a well-researched answer. Richmond has a similar history to that of Cape Town, a history full of interracial hurt, "Jim Crow" apartheid, drug trafficking and violence. In the last few years, we have managed to attract gangs who are taking us to a new level of challenge. Our problems with handgun traffic and murder are well known. But ironically, the George Otis videos which sparked such faith and prayer in South Africa have barely made a stir in Richmond.

It is the purpose of this book to add to a growing dialogue about this intriguing and relevant question: *Why not Richmond?* I want to give my perspective on this question, aware that city leaders in other American cities are struggling with just the same question. In other cities, there are pastors and Christian leaders like myself whom God has led to leave their local ministries and carry prayer burdens for their cities. In this regard, I recommend a book by my friend, Tom White of Corvallis, Oregon, *City-wide Prayer Movements* (Vine Books, 2001). I also recommend Ruth Ruibal's book, *Unity in the Spirit* (TransformNations, 2002, available from the Sentinel Group).

I fervently believe that God has specific plans for the transformation of our city, and of our country as a whole—though, I admit, this transformation looks pretty remote to the naked eye just now.

The Main Thing: Faith in God's Power

The difficulties Richmond faces are no more insoluble than those of Cali or Cape Town. But in Richmond, and in our country generally, we are not used to relying on the power of God. We have grown accustomed to relying on ourselves and solving our own problems. We are no longer too certain whether God would really do anything for us, so we tend to fall back on our own inventiveness to solve all human problems, whether personal or societal. We pray half-heartedly, hoping that God will add His blessing to our ideas and plans. This is Standard Operating Procedure for American Christians. We want God to help us get His work done, but if He doesn't, we believe we can probably succeed anyway.

A Dramatic Shift in Faith 100 Years Ago

This self-confidence is a result of a dramatic shift that happened in America in the last century, which I will trace in Part Four below. It is important to remember how deeply most Americans were prepared to trust the power of God moving through spiritual awakenings prior to that massive paradigm shift.

One hundred and fifty years ago our country was in full-scale debate about how we could keep the power of God flowing and constantly renewing our national life together. These debates grew out of the great spiritual awakenings of our past. Many Christians recognized how important to our country were these seasons we call *awakenings*. To them, the issue was not whether we need God's power to renew our country, but how we can assure that these spiritual awakenings keep happening. Is God waiting on us to do something here? Or does God just decide to bring forth an awakening whenever He wants to? It's just "predestined?"

To show why these debates were so important to that

generation (the first half of the nineteenth century), let me point out just a few of the results of the Second Great Awakening, the most powerful season of spiritual vibrancy in our nation's history. Not only did God tame the most lawless county in the country, Logan County, Kentucky, otherwise known as Rogues' Harbor, He swept the entire nation with Christian fervency for over thirty years. This awakening produced many movements that permanently affected our country, for example, public education, and (as I will show) the abolition of slavery.

By 1860, virtually all the churches had experienced exponential growth. Church membership had grown by nearly three times the population growth rate, despite the fact that the population was growing faster than at any other time in our history. Churches that chose to nurture that awakening showed the greatest growth. Between 1790 and 1860, for example, Methodist churches grew from 700 to 20,000. Presbyterian churches grew from 700 to 6,000. In 1860 there were 35 churches to every bank in our country. Today, there are only four churches for every bank.[2]

What Has Happened to Us?

The America of today bears no relationship to the America of the nineteenth century. Outpourings of God's power are now the hope of the few, mostly of intercessors. While this group of Christians is growing rapidly, for most Americans, the memory of these seasons has faded so completely that nothing remains of it at all. We have no idea that the culture we enjoy is actually a result of previous outpourings of God's power, and that most of our denominations were born at these times. As Dr. J. Edwin Orr has pointed out from a lifetime of research, these seasons of awakening occurred because large numbers of Christians were praying with fervency, unity of the Spirit, and faith in Jesus.

Many Americans are vaguely aware of the great awakenings of our past, but say to themselves, "That was then, but this is now." In other words, that was a rather naïve and provincial period of our history, but now we have to be more broad-minded. Now we must recognize that the world is a very complex place, full of different cultures, and we can't expect God to do the things He did here so long ago. Against that common belief has come the plain fact that God is doing around the world all those same things He used to do among us.

The George Otis videos produced by the Sentinel Group have been particularly effective in bringing this home to us. We begin to realize that we used to have something as a precious treasure, a national heritage. But today, we have lost it, and now other countries have it. I am speaking of the power of God to spiritually awaken whole cities, even whole countries to the goodness and blessing of Jesus Christ.

Historically, Richmond as a city among cities has seemed particularly resistant to spiritual awakenings. In Richmond, more often than not, the awakenings of the past were met with mockery and an attitude of superiority or fear.

In spite of this track record, I believe that God is speaking hope to Richmond and to our nation. His arm is not so shortened, that it cannot save.

Even in saying that, however, there is no question but that our nation is stuck in a place that is far from God, or lukewarm about God. Richmond, in its turn, has had a very unique place as a gateway to the rest of our country. Quite literally, whatever English people brought to the new country came up the James River, was unloaded at Richmond, and spread out from here. In addition, the story of Richmond is central to the history of the country, having a starring role in its deepest agony, the Civil War. We now turn to trace some of that history.

■ ■ ■

Chapter Two

DOMINATION AND CONTROL

When I first came to Richmond, I felt a deep darkness in this city. Trying to understand why a place should be so dark—why some places have such darkness and others do not—has thrown me into a study of history. We are a product of our past, and our past remains with us even when we try to forget it.

Past and Present Are Linked

I have seen this principle in my own personal life. In the last five years, I discovered that my own heart was closed, that I had become very much a mental Christian, speaking the words of a believer, yet my heart often far from God.

One day, I discovered that my heart was full of pain, and this was why I had closed off my heart. This realization took me back to certain experiences I had as a child. As I took stock of my past, and sought the Lord for healing, He began to set me free to new possibilities in my present life and relationships. My heart began to unfreeze. Now I am in a better position to become the person God wants me to be today.

Cities are like that. And I believe something happened to the heart of this city in its childhood—some great tragedy, or rather a great many unhealed and hurtful episodes—and these are hindering our present openness to the Lord today. We need healing, the whole city of us.

Now in the new millennium it is time to come to terms with that wounded history and move beyond it. If we do, we can become more fully the kind of city God wants us to be. And yet, as we pray for this blessing from God, we must recognize that we are up against a darkness that has been in Richmond a very long time.

A Diagnosis

If I could roll it all up into one overarching diagnosis, a sickness with a name to it, I would say that what we are up against is *a spirit of domination and control*. I would like to trace this problem back to its roots. Perhaps you will see what I see as we review the history of Richmond in context with broader Western history.

The historical research reflected in this section came from a desire to understand Richmond's spiritual condition. Today, the term for this sort of research is "spiritual mapping," a term coined, I believe, by George Otis, Jr. If we are to understand the spiritual darkness and/or vibrancy in a city, we must know its past. Demonic power is attracted by certain activities, which, conversely, grieve the Spirit of God. On the other hand, the presence of God is clearly attracted by other opposite behaviors, which invite God's presence and blessing.

Demonic powers tend to stay in a place where they have been welcomed over the centuries. There is a certain basic inertia that takes over a city, inertia for good or for evil. In other words, apart from a dramatic cataclysm, things will keep going in the same direction. Stagnancy reinforces itself. So does worldliness, addictiveness, and so on.

If the life of a city is to change direction, it must be through clear, visionary leadership, sometimes rising out of a cataclysmic event. However, many times in the past the change happened because God gave Christian leaders and intercessors a sense of urgency, and they prevailed on Him to intervene. This is the sort of thing that has created the great awakenings of the past and it has also created a whole new climate in South Africa, as I will show in the final chapter. Cataclysms (such as the Civil War) do not automatically change the spiritual climate of a city. Urgent massive prayer that prevails on God has a much better track record.

In my research, the prevailing spirit over Richmond, for centuries, has been a spirit of domination and control. Richmond was a gateway for this spirit, which spread out from here into the rest of the nation. The pages that follow will focus on the history of this particular form of spiritual darkness, and the harm that it has done to the cause of Christ, to the purposes of God, and to the hope of the city to receive God's blessing to this day.

Jesus and the Sadducees

Let us begin with Jesus, for He should always be the anchor in all our thinking about everything. To comprehend this spirit of domination and control, we begin by recognizing that Jesus confronted this spirit in Jerusalem. The priests of Jerusalem had been called to be in intimate relationship with God. The other non-priestly tribes had received an inheritance of land, but God told the priestly tribe, "I will be your portion." God was bestowing this honor as a special favor, allowing them to praise, pray and give thanks before Him night and day in the temple.

But by Jesus' day this glowing vision of a loving priesthood ministering to the Lord had deteriorated into a system of domination and control. Alfred Edersheim tells us that, by the time of Jesus, the chief priests had:

- abandoned all faith in the power of God,

- formed themselves into a political party, the Sadducees,

- developed political clout by cozying up to Rome,

- developed the temple system into a monopoly to enrich themselves,

- converted money-changing into a system of chicanery,

- multiplied ways to get wealthy Jews to part with their money,

- become the main landowners in the region.[1]

Losing their faith in God, they had turned the temple arena into a system of domination and control, centered around money and political power. They had converted the love of God into a system of vain religion, elevating human tradition to a level of importance that turned God's stomach. This was what Jesus was judging when He overturned the tables of the money-changers. It wasn't just the dishonesty of the money-changers—as though they were a few rotten apples who had found their way into an otherwise righteous sainthood. The whole system, which was supposed to have been a house of prayer, had become a den of domination and control rooted in the love of money. In the end, said Jesus, not one stone would be left on top of another.

The Easy Way Out?

Some people have learned the wrong lesson from this scenario, saying to themselves that the Jews were evil and lost God's blessing, while Christians are now God's priesthood and have replaced the Jews. This "replacement theology" has gotten a foothold in some groups because it is the easy way out. "Christians are the good guys. Jews are the bad guys." By this trick of thought, we Christians avoid having to look at ourselves and see the same seeds of domination and control in us. Neither do we have to acknowledge this same pattern repeating endlessly in the Church throughout the years.

God's people of every age can lose the blessing of God by giving in to the spirit of domination and control. On the other hand, God's people can immunize themselves from that spirit by surrendering their lives to Jesus.

A surrendered life is our only assurance that we ourselves won't end up building systems of domination and control just like the Sadducees. Jesus does not operate through domination and control, but through humility and love. When we accept Him as Savior, we should also accept Him as Lord, then let Him re-make us to be more like Him—to be people of humility and love, not domination and control.

■ ■ ■

Chapter Three

OUR ROOTS IN ENGLAND

Now let's look at Richmond's roots. Look at the place names here in the city—the *James* River and *Henrico* County, for instance. Many of these names take us back to the kings and queens of England and Scotland. Or remember the cross that Christopher Newport planted at the falls of the James, inscribed *"Jacobus Rex, 1607"*—King James, 1607. King James represented a system of domination and control that had grown up in England, and which his representatives were bringing to this country under a very superficial allegiance to Christ. You do not find such names farther north. But they abound in Virginia. "King and Queen County." and "The College of William and Mary," for instance.

A Hostile Take-over of the Church

This system began in earnest with Henry VIII, perhaps the most important king of them all. In an effort to divorce his first wife, Henry decided to name himself "head of the Church" for all English people. In this way, not even Church authorities could get in his way. He became their boss.

Other kings had tried to influence the Church in various ways, going back to Constantine. But what Henry did was new. He hard-wired himself and his heirs into a chain-of-command system of control over the Church. I call this a hostile takeover. I believe Jesus saw it that way too.

Henry's act was a particularly bad idea that short-circuited everything. It entangled two institutions—the Church and the State—like entangling the white and black wires in a household circuit. It has taken centuries to get these two conduits of God's authority untangled again.

Our country has been particularly instrumental in working this problem out. But it was in Scotland and England that the first steps were taken in confronting the terrible confusion of state and church.

The English Church Succumbs

There were some voices of opposition to Henry's plan. Thomas More, a highly respected Roman Catholic Christian, did not follow meekly along. So Henry took off his head. The film, *A Man for All Seasons,* portrays these tragic events. Incidentally, the city where Sir Thomas was tried was called Richmond, the city after which our Richmond was named.

Or consider the tragic end of William Tyndale, whom God called to provide English people with a translation of the Bible into "today's English." This would give them the tools to follow Jesus. But he soon found that Henry, "the head of the Church," did not wish to have the Bible translated into English. In order to continue this important work, Tyndale had to go into hiding. He spent most of his life in hiding; that is why we know so little about him.

Finally lured out of hiding, Tyndale was arrested. Henry tried him and "killed him twice"—first strangling him, then burning him as a public example. Tyndale's last words were: "O Lord, open the King of England's eyes." Tyndale saw the truth. The English Church was being led by a blind man. Fortunately, before he died Tyndale had completed his translation of the Bible.

When English Church leaders saw the price of opposition to Henry's controlling spirit, they quickly fell into line. By this abdication, they began to teach that it is not important whether we Christians follow Jesus or not. It is not important to surrender your life to Him. Christianity is just a religion, a cultural thing for all English people. In that sense, all English people are "Christian" whether they follow Jesus or not—or so many people thought. The meaning of the word Christian began to change.

The Spirit of Domination and Control

What possible reason could have justified Henry in opposing Tyndale's work? Wouldn't God want to have His word more accessible to people—and for the very reasons that drove Tyndale into this work?

Here we must recognize an irony. Many people think of themselves as Christians, while in fact they are motivated and controlled by spiritual powers other than the Spirit of Christ. Dark powers can deceive people who have not fully surrendered their lives to Christ, and Henry had never surrendered his.

There was more here than just a spat between Christians who were not seeing eye-to-eye. There were two entirely different spirits vying for control of the Church and the nation. The spirit of domination and control is the opposite of the Spirit of Christ—always and everywhere it appears. Domination and control are never justified as a way for Christians to behave.

We find in England two very distinct churches–let us boldly say it–a false Church and a true Church. One relies on worldly strength, using dungeons, swords, stranglings and burnings as its weapons—ruling by fear. But terrorism is never Christian.

The true Church relies on God's power in the midst of human weakness. Jesus is its head, and He rules by a spirit of humility and love. His weapons are two—prayer and the word of God.

He is a mighty warrior. Though His weapons are not carnal, they are real weapons, and with them He really does go to war. The Bible tells us that with these weapons he will grind all other kings into the dust, until He alone is King (Daniel 2).

> *Therefore, you kings, be wise;*
> *Be warned, you rulers of the earth.*
> *Serve the Lord with fear*
> *And rejoice with trembling.*
> *Kiss the Son, lest he be angry*
> *And you be destroyed in your way....*
> *(Ps. 2:10-12a)*

The Awakening of Scotland

It was the Scottish whom the Lord first used to oppose the domination and control that had been taking over Christendom in Britain. I believe that Jesus was behind what happened in Scotland because what happened there in the 1520's was the sort of thing that only Jesus can do: He initiated a spiritual awakening using His two weapons.

From the moment William Tyndale's scriptures found their way to Scotland, they ignited fires in the hearts of the Scottish people. One man, George Wishart, took this fresh translation and began to preach God's word in the open air. When he did, hardened criminals, notorious people, would suddenly be seized with conviction and converted in a moment. For example, John Knox later recalled:

> *(Wishart) continued preaching more than three hours. In that sermon God wrought so wonderfully with him that one of the most wicked men that was in that country, named Laurence Rankin, laird of Shiel, was converted. The tears ran from his eyes in such abundance that all men wondered. His conversion was without hypocrisy, for his life and conversation witnessed it in all times to come.*[1]

This is the sort of thing that no denominational executive can decree, no committee can plan. What was happening in Scotland was not just a good idea. It was a God idea. A Jesus idea. In those days, spiritual awakening became so common in Scotland that one historian wrote: "The Church of Scotland hath been singular among the churches. ...Whereas in other nations the Lord thought it enough to convict a few in a city, village, or family to himself, leaving the greater part in darkness, in Scotland the whole nation was converted by lump...."[2]

This description is a bit of an exaggeration. The awakening affected mainly the Scottish lowlands, to the south and east, and was less influential in the highlands. Still, this historian was describing a new historical reality, the power of God in seasons of great awakening. This was perhaps the first modern great awakening.

John Knox

George Wishart attracted a good deal of attention. John Knox, a Catholic priest at the time, became so fascinated with what God was doing that he made himself Wishart's bodyguard. Knox was good with a sword.

Wishart also attracted the attention of the system of domination and control that was operating in Scotland at the time. This had grown up under the authority of the various Jacobite kings, especially James V, father of Mary, Queen of Scots. As in England, we see two churches, one using prayer and the word of God, the other using armies and dungeons. (If we were to trace the history of Britain through, we would see this pattern over and over again. We would see it in successive awakenings among Puritans and Pilgrim separatists in England, and in the Quaker revival of the 1650's. All believed in the weapons of Christ, and all were opposed with weapons of domination and control by the state-controlled Church.)

Knox, along with a good many other Scottish lowlanders, switched from the false Church to the true Church. The new Reformers formed a community at St. Andrews castle. But Cardinal Beaton, under the authority of the Scottish king, forced his way into the castle and arrested all the Reformers. John Knox, like many others, was sentenced to 19 months as a slave. This sentence in the galley of a ship very nearly killed him and broke his health permanently. In later years, as a preacher at St. Giles cathedral in Edinburgh, he had to be helped up to the pulpit. In this weakness, Knox had to give up the sword as a weapon, and use only the weapons of Christ. In his later years, Mary, Queen of Scots was heard to say, "I fear the prayers of John Knox more than all the armies of England."

After his term as a galley slave, Knox lived in England for five years. Knowing that Henry VIII had broken away from the domineering influence of the Roman Catholic Church of his day, Knox hoped to bask in the freedom of the English Reformation. What he discovered there was a disappointment, to say the least. He found just another system of domination and control, which severely constrained prayer and the word of God.

After five years, he went to Geneva, where he got to know John Calvin. Calvin gave him the doctrinal framework on which to hang his experience of God. Calvin was also a man of intense prayer and impassioned heart.

John Knox returned to Scotland to provide leadership to the continued awakening of his country. He described this season:

God did so multiply our number that it appeared as if men had rained from the clouds.[3]

The thirst of the poor people, as well as of the nobility here, is wondrous great, which putteth me in comfort that Christ Jesus shall triumph for a space here, in the north and extreme parts of the earth.[4]

The Triumph of Christ

Christ did triumph. Out of that awakening, the Scottish people learned that, for Jesus' sake, they had to oppose *all* systems of domination and control. You cannot serve two masters, and you cannot have two kings. "God alone is Lord of the conscience" became their motto.

To stand for this principle out of reverence for Christ was costly. John Welch, the son-in-law of Knox (a great intercessor who prayed eight hours a day), was captured by James V and imprisoned at Blackness castle for over a year. I have been there. The latrines of the living quarters drain through the courtyard into the dungeon where Welch was imprisoned.

As the years passed the Scottish who had been touched by the awakening formed covenants of resistance, and so became known as Covenanters. I have visited Dunottar castle where over 100 Covenanters were packed like sardines into a cell and left to die. After a few months, the few who had survived were sold into slavery.

What Good Did It Do?

During those years the awakened Scots turned back to Tyndale's translation of the Bible to look for a way of challenging the spirit of domination and control. They created a non-hierarchical form of Church government, based on the principle of a gathered community of leaders "subject to one another out of reverence for Christ" (Eph. 5:21). These they called "elders" (*presbuteroi*) and the new type of church government was called presbyterian. Its purpose was to resist the abuse of power, which seemed to have taken over churches.

They also developed their parliaments into a real alternative to royalty as a way to govern nations—directly challenging the Jacobite kings and queens that had taken control of Scotland. The new ideas of Christian freedom that resulted spread southward and began to attack the whole concept of domination by English kings as well. Their Bibles said, "It is for freedom that Christ has set us free. Stand firm, then, and do not let yourselves be burdened again by a yoke of slavery" (Gal. 5:1).

Our Western ideas of freedom came from these successive Christian awakenings in Scotland and England. I am trying to demonstrate that there is a direct connection between the movement of the Spirit of God in Christian awakenings, and the basic concepts of freedom that we cherish in the West. The one caused the other. Jesus wanted His people free. God had warned His people about worldly kings at the beginning of Israel's monarchy (in 1 Sam. 8). Kings were never His idea. Unfortunately, neither Scotland nor England was destined to free itself from the spirit of domination and control in the monarchy apart from a civil war in each country.

A Brief Warning

Before we move on to see how these roots affected Richmond, let me give a word of explanation and caution.

In the period I am describing, the French Catholic and Anglican Churches come out looking quite bad, really. It would be easy to conclude that Catholics and Anglicans are not good Christians. But this would be a false conclusion.

It is true. At that period, these two churches were not at their best. But it is more complicated than that. The Bible tells us that we wage war against spiritual principalities and powers, not against flesh and blood. Our enemy is never a denomination or a person (such as a king). Our true enemy is always principalities that are trying to infiltrate the Church and deceive us into opposing or replacing Christ. Paul's warning is, "Watch yourself, or you also may be tempted" (Gal. 6:1b). I repeat: all of us are vulnerable to the invasion and infestation of this spirit. The only sure way of protecting ourselves is to fully surrender our lives to Jesus, who is God's anointed one. When we accept Him as Savior, we should also accept Him as Lord.

Again, it is easy to adopt a "bad-guys, good-guys" mentality when studying our roots. As we try to speak the truth about our past, we must avoid this easy trap.

I have been to Scotland several times, and have overheard some anti-Catholic sentiment there. No doubt, these feelings are based on wounds of the past, maybe going back to the days of the Covenanters. The Bible tells us how the root of bitterness "defiles many" (Heb. 12:15). If bitterness is not cleansed out through forgiveness, it will cause a victimized person to repeat the same sins of domination and control that have victimized him. The victim becomes the perpetrator.

This may be what happened, for example, when the Puritan, Oliver Cromwell, finally defeated King Charles, as portrayed in the film *Cromwell*. Puritans had been persecuted for over a century, and Cromwell's victory should be an occasion we remember fondly to this day. Unfortunately, Cromwell fell into the very same spirit of domination and control that he had opposed in others.

The same tragedy occurred during the French Revolution. Victims became perpetrators, and made the guillotine infamous to this day.

Before we trace the influence of the spirit of domination and control in Richmond, let's focus in on one particularly relevant form of it for Richmond—slavery.

■ ■ ■

Chapter Four

THE SLAVE TRADE

I have tried to show a connection between Christian awakening and the emergence of freedom and democracy. Many people today seem unaware of this connection, so central to our national identity. They think that democracy just happened. I say it was a gift of God through Jesus Christ, the mighty warrior.

But even more relevant to Richmond's roots is the connection between Christian awakening and the abolition of slavery. Totalitarianism and slavery are two institutions that flow from the same spirit, the spirit of domination and control. Is it so surprising that Christ, who opposed the abuse of power under English and Scottish monarchies, would also want to destroy slavery? The two issues grew up on parallel tracks connected to each other. Where the one flourished, so did the other.

The slavery issue strikes at the heart of what Richmond became in its earlier years, and it is the most relevant issue in helping us understand the spiritual darkness over this city.

My Assumptions

In this brief study, I am making two assumptions. These are my own personal biases. First, I believe that history is "His story." This is God's world we live in, and Jesus is in control of its history. "All authority in heaven and on earth has been given to me," He said. I believe this. Jesus will come back at the end of the age, and we will all see how in control He has been all along, even when it did not seem so.

My second assumption is this. I believe that God most clearly reveals His will and His heart during seasons of spiritual awakening. History resembles one of those Japanese waterfalls made of bamboo—you see them in Japanese gardens. Water pours into a bamboo bucket until the bucket is filled to the top. Then the lever tips the bucket down, and all the water pours out, and the bucket returns to its original position.

I do not claim to understand why we have seen this pattern throughout history, but the pattern is there, whether you can explain it or not. We go through seasons in which God hides Himself, apparently using hiddenness for His own good purposes. At other times, He chooses to manifest His power, glory and love more openly. Then we can see Him and His intentions more clearly. God shows us more clearly who He is and what He stands for: love. He takes us up in His arms of love, and He also demands that we learn the ways of love. God's word is a two-edged sword. If we receive grace from Him, then we are also required to give it and live it.

The Other Edge of the Sword

People during seasons of awakening get to know the grief in God's heart caused by sin, by our lovelessness. There has always been a great deal of weeping at such times. Some of this weeping has to do with personal sin, and some from corporate sin. This personal awareness of God's heart becomes a key factor in the progress of history, for example, in the history of slavery, a corporate sin.

In times of hiddenness, God allows a great deal to go wrong with us. He is allowing us to learn from our mistakes. He has spoken His word, but we have chosen to ignore it, go our own way, and learn from our mistakes by experiencing pain. This He calls judgment. Judgment is nothing more nor less than God saying, "Don't I know best after all? Wouldn't your life be more content and enjoyable if you would learn my ways at last?"

In times of God's hiddenness, we love to compartmentalize our lives. We say to ourselves: "This area is *sacred*, where God belongs, but that is *secular*, where I can do whatever I want." "This area is *private and spiritual*, the place where I relate to God; that area is public and political and that is the real world." "This is my *Church*, the place where I learn about God; but that is *reality*, where I have to actually live."

During seasons of awakening, we cannot get away with this sort of compartmentalizing. We suddenly become aware that Christ is Lord of *everything* and the little mental tricks we play in compartmentalizing Him out of nine-tenths of our lives don't work during these seasons. He comes out of hiding carrying a winnowing fork, and He begins to separate, sift and winnow His world. In times of awakening, we have to either have Him in all of our compartments, or in none of them. Jesus is an all-or-nothing kind of guy. We see this more clearly during spiritual awakenings.

World history in the A.D. era consists of seasons when Jesus has come out of hiding to awaken large numbers of people to His presence and power. Few of us Americans have experienced this in our lifetime. During a spiritual awakening, Christ asserts Himself over all of life: public and private, church and corporation, interior and exterior. He dismantles our silly separations between "sacred" and "secular."

That is why awakened Christians looked at the hypocrisies of aristocrats perpetrating barbarities on their fellow human beings and were appalled that such people could call themselves Christians and attend Christian churches. This sort of thing happened a great deal in the years following Henry VIII. Those who had been awakened were appalled at the resulting condition of the

Anglican state-controlled churches. Eventually awakened English people divided themselves into two groups: Puritans, who thought there was hope for the state-controlled Anglican church, and Pilgrims or Separatists, who did not.

The Evil of the African Slave Trade

One example of the falsity and grievous immorality these awakened Christians began to point out had to do with slavery. We can see already that many of them had suffered from being enslaved. It is not hard to see why many did not go along with a new development in England toward the end of the 16th century–the African slave trade.

There had always been slavery. It was everywhere. For instance, there was slavery on this continent among Native people. When Lewis and Clark traveled West on their Voyage of Discovery, they picked up a slave woman named Sacajawea among the Hidatsas and returned her to her own people, the Shoshones. Many other examples of slavery could be mentioned.

But the form of slavery that was developed out of Portugal, spreading into England and then America, which formed a slave bridge between Africa and the New World, was a particularly cruel, destructive and evil form of it. Richmond was a center of this evil. Consider the views expressed by John Wesley, founder of the Methodist Church, in a letter to William Wilberforce commending him for his extremely courageous work in opposing the African slave trade.

> *...Unless God has raised you up for this very thing, you will be worn out by the opposition of men and devils: but if God be for you who can be against you? Are all of them together stronger than God? Oh, be not weary of well-doing. Go on in the name of God, and in the power of His might, till even American slavery, the vilest that ever saw the sun, shall vanish away before it.*[1]

This evil had been perpetrated by the Catholic Church (with official blessing from the Pope) beginning in Portugal. It then spread to England in the wake of the reign of Henry VIII. It is my belief that when the Christian Church abdicates authority to a spirit of domination and control, the nation loses the blessings of God that would have flowed through the people of God into the nation. Instead, curses are free to grow up in the life of that nation, as also in the Church.

True Evil

My friend, David Pott, organizer of the Lifeline Expedition that came to Richmond in October, 2004, did a great deal of research on the Portuguese and English slave trade. He writes:

> *In 1562, Sir John Hawkins sailed from Plymouth to West Africa. His flagship was* The Jesus of Lubeck *and it was on this voyage that slaves were first taken by Englishmen to the New World....What an irony that the first*

*English vessel to take slaves should be called by
the name of Him who came "to release the
captives" and that Hawkins' personal standard
was a bound African woman! On another slaving
voyage, Hawkins captured a Portuguese slave
ship and renamed it* The Grace of God *before he
continued his business.*[2]

These people used the name of Jesus shamelessly, seemingly unaware that there was anything evil about what they were doing. Though they tacked the name of Jesus on their ships, on the inside a spirit of domination and control had taken over their personalities, their businesses and their very lives. It is for such as these that Jesus says: "Not everyone who says to me, 'Lord, Lord,' will enter the kingdom of heaven, but only he who does the will of my Father who is in heaven" (Mt. 7:21). We see here the disaster that happens when we teach that people can be saved without embracing the lordship of Christ. It is this sort of blatant evil creeping into the Church that led awakened Christians to distance themselves from the State-controlled Church.

Some of the worst evils in history have been perpetrated by "Christians" who never surrendered their lives to the Lord of history. Of course, all of us have made this surrender imperfectly; we all struggle with areas of disobedience and fear. But that is very different from what we are describing here—people who never gave a single thought to turning their lives over to Jesus to learn what pleases Him.

The England-Africa-Virginia Triangle

In England, the slave trade was developed by Birmingham manufacturers of firearms, who wanted to find a market for their wares. England found this market all over the world, but particularly in Africa. By 1788 there were 4,000 gun makers in Birmingham and 100,000 guns a year going to slave traders.

Tribal chiefs, faced with a revolution in weaponry, were in the position of either accepting the slave-for-weapons trade offered by English traders—or seeing the weapons go to competing tribal chiefs. This was the African version of street gangs. It was a no-win situation for them.[3] What did they have that English traders wanted as trade goods? Slaves. So they began to fight other tribes, looking for people to trade in return for guns, which enabled them to gain more slaves.

In 2001, Africans produced a film, *Adanggaman*, which portrays African complicity in the slave trade. In all candor, though, the initiative was with the English and other European gun traffickers, especially the Dutch, French and Portuguese. By the 18th century, Europeans sold between 283,000 and 394,000 guns annually to West African tribal chiefs.

During the four centuries of the African slave trade, between 11 and 15 million Africans were transported to this continent. Three million slaves perished on the ships across the Atlantic, and that number does not include the millions slain in slave-taking battles in Africa, nor the many others who lost their lives here after the voyage. One representative of the Royal Africa Company watched an inter-tribal battle that resulted in 8,000 captives sold into slavery, and dead bodies so crimson with blood that "if it had rained blood, it could not have lain thicker on the ground."

Prior to the great awakenings in this country, slavery spread to all the American colonies. It was certainly not just a Southern phenomenon. There were slave ports in Boston, New York and Providence, as well as in Richmond, Charleston and Savannah. Slavery was everywhere.

John Newton

Much of the evil of this system lies in what it did to the English slavers themselves. John Newton, who was later converted to Christ, looked back on his slave trading days reflecting: "The real or supposed necessity of treating the Negroes with rigour gradually brings a numbness upon the heart and renders those who are engaged in it too indifferent to the sufferings of their fellow-creatures."[4] This awakening of compassion in a former slaver, this revulsion about his former desensitized condition, shows the power of spiritual awakening to rebuild an interior sensitivity to basic right and wrong. No one is so evil or so lost that he cannot repent when Jesus awakens him. The hymn, "Amazing Grace," in which Newton wrote "I once was blind but now I see," describes this God-ordained power of spiritual awakening. This hymn has become a sort of national hymn in two countries, America and Scotland. It reflects a long history of spiritual awakenings that have often occurred simultaneously in the two countries.

Unfortunately, as I will show, most Richmonders were unacquainted with this power and resisted it. But before I show this unfortunate track record, let me show more broadly the track record of Jesus Christ in confronting this vile commerce. Then we will look more closely at Richmond's historic roots in it—and why Richmond so often resisted the awakenings of God.

■ ■ ■

Chapter Five

JESUS GOES TO WAR

Jesus was putting on His armor against this form of evil. He kept on coming out of hiding during seasons of awakening, and each season brought greater indignation against slavery. Each awakening increased the volume of God's voice: "*You must not do this!*" Some Christians listened. Others did not. But the facts of the case are a matter of record. Christian awakenings were the main factor in the demise of the slave industry, as Jesus waged war against the spirit of domination and control. Let us review that record now.

The Quakers

Let's begin with the Revival that took place in the 1650's, just as the British slave trade was getting under way. That was the first awakening following the beginnings of the colonizing of this country in 1607 at Jamestown and in 1620 at Plymouth, Massachusetts. It was the awakening that produced the Society of Friends, otherwise known as Quakers.

There were many English believers who saw that the English Church was a corrupt system of self-protection. They wanted to rediscover a purer, more scriptural kind of Christianity. They wanted to restore the Church to its original simplicity. George Fox became the torchbearer of this movement.

Fox told his people to come together quite simply to listen to God. No liturgies. No rituals. And no clergymen to shatter the silence in which God would speak with His still small voice to people with open hearts. We need no priest but Jesus, Fox said. Jesus died to become our one mediator. We need no other.

Now here's the point. What did they hear God say when they opened their ears to that still small voice? They heard Him say, "I hate slavery." Early in the game, certain Quakers became involved in the slave trade, it is true. But the Society of Friends recognized that this was intolerable to Jesus, *because they were listening to Him*.

And that is why the Society of Friends were among the first to devote themselves to the abolition of slavery. For the next two hundred years, from 1650 to 1850, they hammered away at slavery—a tiny minority in a world that had always had slavery. You could put one Quaker in a room full of people, and he or she would always oppose slavery. Why? Because they had heard the grief and indignation in the heart of God.

But let's move on. We want to get the broad sweep of God's dealings on the slave trade.

The Great Awakening

The next season of awakening began among the Moravians of Saxony, in eastern Germany. The Moravians were the spiritual progeny of John Hus, one of the first Protestant martyrs.

In 1712, Count Nicholaus Ludwig von Zinzendorf invited persecuted Christians from all over Europe to find shelter on his estate in Saxony. But when they arrived, these believers turned his peaceful estate into a cauldron of discord. They could not stop arguing over doctrines and practices they had learned in their separate traditions.

In desperation, the Count gathered the bickering saints together and made them sign a covenant of unity. He also divided them into prayer watch teams, and assigned each team one hour per day to pray. No hour of any day was to be without prayer. He designated one location on his estate as a place to gather for prayer, called Herrnhut, the Watchtower of the Lord. Immediately, all bickering stopped as these believers descended from their heads to their hearts and gained the heart of Jesus.

As these Christians prayed, God continually poured out blessings, not once, but many times. For example, at noon on August 10, 1727,

> *while pastor Rothe was holding the meeting at Herrnhut, he felt himself overwhelmed by a wonderful and irresistible power of the Lord and sank down into the dust before God, and with him sank down the whole assembled congregation, in an ecstasy of feeling. In this frame of mind they continued till midnight, engaged in praying and singing, weeping and supplication.*[1]

So fired up were the Moravians with this heart-to-heart time with God that, when they eventually moved from the community on their various missions (called out in obedience to prayer), they continued faithful to their watch assignments all over the world. It is said that the Moravian prayer watch lasted a hundred years.

The Results of the Watch

What was the result of this prayer watch? What good did it do, besides stop some bickering among strong-willed Christians, and make a few people feel better about themselves?

First, as these teams waited on the Lord, Jesus began to give them His heart for suffering people, especially for black slaves on plantations in the West Indies. Fired up by the compassionate heart of Jesus, two awakened believers, Leonard Dober and David Nitschmann, ventured across the Atlantic to bring the gospel to the slaves of St. Thomas Island. They were willing to become slaves if necessary, to communicate the loving heart of Christ to those in this darkness.

Soon a steady stream of Moravians hazarded the ocean voyage to bring the gospel to those slaves. There is little doubt that the descendants of many black slaves in this country gained their Christian faith from these Moravians. Many of these trans-national evangelists died young in the process of fulfilling that calling, but they had been awakened to Christ, and they were ready to die for Him. This was the literal beginning of the modern missions movement, and it began when some intercessors gained God's heart for black slaves.

The Moravian prayer also birthed the Great Awakening. On New Year's Day, 1739, there were sixty Moravians present at the love feast on Fetter Lane in London, together with seven Anglican clergy, including John and Charles Wesley and George Whitefield. Of that meeting Wesley writes:

About three in the morning, as we were continuing instant in prayer, the power of God came mightily upon us, insomuch that many cried for exceeding joy, and many fell to the ground. As soon as we were recovered a little from that awe and amazement at the presence of His Majesty, we broke out with one voice—"We praise Thee, O God; we acknowledge Thee to be the Lord!"[2]

The Clapham Awakening

But let's move on. The next season of awakening was known as the Second Great Awakening, and it seems to have lasted 35 years or so. During that season, God dramatically upped the volume of His voice on the abolition of slavery so that more and more people could hear it. Most Americans knew that this issue was trouble and didn't want to hear about it. They just wanted the issue to go away.

In England, the spiritual awakening at this season was called the Clapham Revival. Very often, there is a direct parallel between awakenings in Britain and those in America. God touched Clapham, a neighborhood of London full of some of England's most influential men and women—members of Parliament and business leaders. Among these was William Wilberforce, a stub of a man barely five feet tall, who was so convicted by the heart of God toward slavery that he devoted the rest of his life to eradicating it from the British Commonwealth. He succeeded in 1833. (And when his work was done, he died three days later.)

Some of Wilberforce's neighbors were business leaders. One, a man named Harrison, was a director of the Hudson's Bay Company, whose influence extended around the world. He used his position to strongly discourage slavery here on this continent among Native tribes, especially among the Chinooks, who practiced a particularly brutal form of slavery against their neighboring tribes on the Columbia River. But that was the West coast.

Here in the East, the Second Great Awakening in America began in 1799 with the Kentucky Revival and transitioned into the Finney Revival of the 1830's. By the time Wilberforce had eradicated slavery with an edict of Parliament on July 26, 1833, abolitionists like John Greenleaf Whittier were ready to establish the American Anti-Slavery Society that same December. This Society, for the first time, refused to succumb to the universal complaint, "Slavery's bad, but what can you do?" The roots of this movement, as usual, grew up among awakened Christians, as William Lee Miller summarizes:

The new abolitionism had its most energetic support in the areas where the revivalism of the time was strongest...

At the center of the new abolitionism were young Presbyterian and Congregational ministers of a trailblazing sort...

...Perhaps "ministers" is not the right word for them. Many were indeed converted in some high-octane religious setting; did go to seminaries; were ordained. They all did make their antislavery case in distinctly Christian terms—very much so. They did indeed have the style and approach of the preacher or evangelist. Nevertheless they characteristically did not serve churches. They traveled; they spoke; they wrote; they distributed tracts; they edited journals; they agitated; they were mobbed. They did those things full-time.

That was their job. That was almost their denomination, their community of faith.[3]

Miller's book, *Arguing about Slavery*, is a must for anyone who wants to look into the roots of the Civil War. For a somewhat shorter summary of the heroic deeds of these Christian leaders, I recommend *Sounding Forth the Trumpet* by Peter Marshall and David Manuel. They tell the story of the start of the Ohio State Anti-Slavery Society by Theodore Dwight Weld, one of the converts of the Finney revivals. Weld chose one of the most anti-abolitionist towns of them all to begin his abolitionist work: Zanesville, Ohio.

... Weld got there three weeks early—only to find the town shut up tight against him. As he wryly noted, he could not find "even a shanty." He removed to the town of Putnam across the Muskingum River, where he did find a hall. But when he began to lecture in it, a mob from Zanesville broke the windows and tore the gate off. When Weld finished and came out, they stoned and clubbed him, and the alarmed custodians of the hall closed it.

At this point even the bravest of men might wonder if he had truly heard God. Weld never doubted. Finding another hall, he suffered similar maltreatment until at last one night the mob listened. The next night he was given a pulpit. Then the good people of Zanesville pleaded with him to come back

*across the river. Sixteen nights later, hundreds rose to
commit themselves to abolition.*[4]

In the first half of the Nineteenth Century, God was
turning up the heat on slavery, and the spirit of domination
and control that undergirded it.

The Prayer Awakening of 1857-1858

The Second Great Awakening died out somewhere in
the late 1830's—or at least, Charles Finney complained of
this. But God had not disappeared from the scene. In 1857,
God provoked a great prayer awakening in this country.

In 1857, Dr. John Lafayette Girardeau was the 30-
year-old pastor of Anson Street Presbyterian Church in
Charleston, a church of 48 black members, mostly slaves,
and 12 whites. Frustrated by the powerlessness of his
preaching and the lack of results in ministry, Girardeau
announced to his little congregation that he would not
preach another sermon until God poured out His Spirit.
Intensive prayer replaced the preaching of God's word
for months on end, until one day the pastor felt a
mysterious current of God's power flowing through him.
Then he announced, "The Holy Spirit has come.
Preaching begins tomorrow."

Thousands flocked to Anson Street and were converted.
As a result, a mysterious Spirit of prayer raced up and down
the coast, especially among slaves. Slaves began to pray with
an unaccountable intensity and fervency.

In Virginia, this movement took the form of "kettle" prayers. The slaves, aware that their masters did not wish to have them praying fervently, would place barrels or kettles over their heads so that they could pray with liberty without being heard by their white masters. The barrel became their prayer closet, a way to "shut the door" as Jesus had commanded for those who "pray in secret."

This intensity of prayer among slaves continued right through the years of the Civil War. Virginius Dabney says that great numbers of slaves prayed quietly for a Northern victory. Few historians recognize the importance of this fifth-column activity, which was leveled against the spirit of domination and control in Richmond.

Throughout the North, this prayer awakening took root first in New York (where the main leader was Jeremiah Lanphier, a Dutch Reformed Christian) and spread as far west as Omaha.

The Passion of William Seymour

We move now to the most recent of the great spiritual awakenings in this country: the Azusa Street Revival that produced the Pentecostal denominations. Beginning in 1900, God had led a great many Christians, among them R.A. Torrey of the Moody Bible Institute, to pray for something no one had thought of yet: a worldwide spiritual awakening. The prayers of these and countless other saints were answered beginning about 1903 with the great Welsh Revival, which spread around the world to India, China, Korea and Europe.

In this country the long-sought awakening started in Los Angeles, California, at a storefront church on Azusa Street. And whom did God choose to lead this great awakening? His choice was William Seymour, the son of a slave, a black man with little or no education, only one good eye, and a massive love for Jesus—a man who had allowed Jesus to get into his heart.

This choice may seem incomprehensible to those who do not know God's heart as He had revealed it through history. There were so many credentialed and educated white church leaders, people whose theology and doctrine were well buttoned down, men who held the respect of the established Christian Church. Why didn't God choose one of those: a Jonathan Edwards or a Samuel Davies or a Lyman Beecher or even a Charles Finney?

The answer? God surely wanted to make a statement about us Americans—a statement that confronted us with our narrow attitudes and our restrictive love. He was proclaiming, in this choice of leaders, the width, height, length and breadth of His love, which is for people of all races, cultures, languages and tribes. This choice, in other words, was God's response to Jim Crow, that bitterly racist pattern of domination and control that grew up after the Civil War.

Azusa Street produced the Pentecostal denominations. Those denominations have emphasized the gifts of the

Spirit, especially the gift of tongues. But there were two gifts, not just one, that William Seymour believed God was giving through the Azusa Street Revival. As Harvey Cox summarized in his book, *Fire from Heaven*:

> *...for Seymour, in a segregated America, God was now assembling a new and racially inclusive people to glorify his name and to save a Jim Crow nation lost in sin.*
>
> *In retrospect the interracial character of the growing congregation on Azusa Street was indeed a kind of miracle. It was, after all, 1906, a time of growing, not diminishing, racial separation everywhere else. But many visitors reported that in the Azusa Street revival blacks and whites and Asians and Mexicans sang and prayed together.*
>
> *...A southern white preacher later jotted in his diary that he was first offended and startled, then inspired, by the fact that, as he put it, "the color line was washed away by the blood."[5]*

What was being confronted was not only the separation of the races, but the spirit of white supremacy that lay behind the separation. It was only the latest skirmish in a battle between the love of Jesus Christ and the spirit of domination and control.

To Summarize

Let me summarize this chapter. There were five major spiritual awakenings between the 17th and the 20th centuries. Each is known for emphasizing a different gift God restored to the Body of Christ:

1. The Quakers, 1650's. God restored the inner "still small voice" of God.

2. The Great Awakening, 1730's. God began the modern missions movement.

3. The Second Great Awakening, early 1800's. God emphasized repentance from corporate sin.

4. The Prayer Awakening of 1857-1858. God brought widespread prayer.

5. The Azusa Street Revival of 1905. God restored the gifts and power of the Holy Spirit for ministry.

Each of these movements brought a distinct gift "so that no good gift would be lacking." But in and through every single one of the massive awakenings, there is a consistent hammering away at the slavery issue, revealed in different ways. Each awakening turned up the volume of God's voice—"Slavery is not my will." Each generation of awakened Christians produced the main leadership that forced the issue for everyone. And always, this was through the two weapons of Christ: prayer and the word of God.

If we accept that God has expressed Himself most clearly through spiritual awakenings, we must conclude that it was God—Jesus, that is—who destroyed slavery, just as it was Jesus who destroyed the abuse of power by the aristocracy. This is what I say: Jesus is a mighty warrior, and when He truly goes to battle, victory is inevitable.

■ ■ ■

Part Two

RICHMOND'S TRAGIC LOVE AFFAIR
WITH THE SPIRIT OF
DOMINATION AND CONTROL

Chapter Six

RICHMOND BEFORE
THE GREAT AWAKENING

Now we are ready to trace Richmond's spiritual roots, growing deep into the soil of spiritual conflict in England 400 years ago. This is especially urgent and meaningful as we approach the 400th anniversary of the founding of the Virginia Colony at Jamestown, which corresponded to the very first English settlements at Dutch Gap and Fulton Hill.

The first Europeans who came to these shores were entirely British Protestants of one sort or another. Even as late as 1860, the non-Native population of this country was 70% English Protestant.[1] But there were two distinctly different groups of British people who came to these shores in the beginning. One went north. The other went south. Those who came to the northern colonies were primarily religious refugees. Their purpose for coming here was highly Christian, as reflected, for instance, in Governor

William Bradford's book, *Of Plimouth Plantation*. Bradford gave four reasons for the journey across the Atlantic:

1. To avoid the extreme discouragements and hardships of the Old Country,

2. Merely to survive as a community of Christians,

3. To shield their children from an increasingly worldly culture,

4. To "advance the gospel of the kingdom of Christ in those remote parts." [2]

Wave after wave of religious refugees settled in the northern colonies motivated by similar hopes. First were the "Pilgrim" Separatists who set foot on Plymouth Rock in 1620. After them came the Puritans, who settled in Connecticut and Massachusetts west of where the Pilgrims had settled at Cape Cod. Then came the Quakers, the Society of Friends, who settled in Rhode Island and Pennsylvania, to the West of the Puritans. Then came the Presbyterians, after a significant detour in Ireland. Scottish-Irish Presbyterians settled to the West of the Quakers in New Jersey and Pennsylvania—and then began to move south into Virginia, down what is now the I-81 corridor.

Beginnings of Richmond

It was a very different group of people who first emigrated to Virginia and the South beginning in 1607.

Christopher Newport sailed up the James River from Jamestown and planted a wooden cross here at the heart of what would become Richmond. This cross, however, was not planted in the name of Jesus, but in the name of King James. The difference in allegiance is very significant, in that they did not see any conflict of interest between James and Jesus.

To get a feel for the spirit of what was planted here, look at Sir Thomas Dale, the leader of the little community of Henricus (or Henrico) at Dutch Gap, just south of Richmond. Virginius Dabney described him: "Dale, a stern disciplinarian, even for that era when Draconian punishments were commonplace, did not hesitate to torture or put to death those who disobeyed his edicts."[3] Dale, though a Puritan, was infected with a spirit of domination and control.

Contrast his style with that of Governor John Winthrop of the Massachusetts Bay Colony, author of "A Model of Christian Charity," which said, "that every man might have need of others, and from hence they might be all knit more nearly together in the bond of brotherly affection."[4]

Of course, there were men of true Christian spirit involved in the founding of Virginia. One, for example, was Sir Edwin Sandys, leader of the Reformation Anglicans in the House of Commons and longtime friend of the Separatists who sailed on the Mayflower as "Pilgrims." Unfortunately, Sandys was illegally imprisoned by James I, who eventually crushed the Virginia Company itself in 1624. Sandys not only promoted representative government, but, as a Christian, promoted education in the form of "Henricus Colledge" in 1619, the first official school in this country. This school was also crushed by James I. A bill to revive the school in 1660 was vetoed by Governor Berkeley of Virginia, who feared that the common rabble would not be able to handle literacy.

By and large, the founders of the Virginia colony were not motivated by Christian principles, but were looking for gold and for a passage through to India. They were, in their own way, *conquistadores*, possessing a different spirit than those who migrated to the North who were mostly refugees from the State-controlled Church. What established itself here *was* the State-controlled Church.

State-controlled Church

It is difficult for us today to appreciate what a state-controlled Church was like, because the whole idea has been so thoroughly discredited today. We are speaking of clergy paid by the State, who used the laws of the State to force people to come to church, to pray in certain ways and to tithe. (By this time, at least, they had given up trying to keep the Bible from being published.)

Sabbath-breaking became an offense punishable by law. If you failed to show up at church on a Sunday, you would likely be arrested, placed in the stocks at the center of town and exposed to public ridicule. If you were a repeat offender, they might well nail your ears to the wood of the stocks and throw garbage at you.

This is the gospel according to the spirit of domination and control. The clergy believed in this system because they profited from it. Any threat to the system was taken to court and punished with fines, imprisonment and various creative ways of degrading people. These clergymen really thought that this is Christianity. Most of us today know that it is a form of religion that has been twisted beyond all recognition from what Jesus intended or established.

As in England the greatest threat to this system was from that despised class of Christians known as "dissenters"—that is, awakened Christians. They persecuted these people with the same carnal weapons they had used in England. Who were these dissenters? They were the non-Anglican Christians who had emigrated from England to the Northern colonies. For example, here is an official proclamation of Governor William Gooch of Williamsburg:

A PROCLAMATION

Whereas It is represented to me that several Itinerant Preachers have lately Crept into the Colony and that the Suffering these Corrupters of our faith and true Religion do to propagate their Shocking Doctrines may be of mischievous

> *consequences. I have, therefore, thought fit, by*
> *and with the Advice of his Majesty's Council,*
> *to issue the Proclamation strictly requiring all*
> *Magistrates and officers to discourage and*
> *prohibit, as far as they legally can, All Itinerant*
> *Preachers, whether New-Light Presbyterians,*
> *Moravians, or Methodists, from Teaching,*
> *Preaching or holding any meeting in this Colony.*
> *And that all Persons be enjoined to be aiding*
> *and assisting in that purpose.*
>
> > *Given under my Hand at Williamsburg this*
> > *third day of April, 1747 and in the xx^{th} year*
> > *of his Majesty's Reign.*
> > > *William Gooch*
> > > *God Save the King*[5]

William Gooch was one of the gentler, kinder souls in Virginia. Much more combative was Patrick Henry, the uncle of the man you and I remember under that name (who made the famous speech, "Give me liberty or give me death.") This uncle was true to form for the spirit of his times, a priest of the State-controlled Church who had anything but liberty on his mind. And his brother, John Henry, young Patrick's dad, was the Sheriff, whose job it was to arrest dissenters and present them before the courts to receive punishment for their rebellion against "true religion."

William Byrd and Church Hill

During that first 140 years, the problem of domination and control in the name of Christ infected Virginia at its deepest roots. This showed up in three areas; the aristocracy, African slavery, and the State-controlled Church.

In 1733, much of the land in this area was owned by William Byrd II. Byrd owned, in true aristocratic fashion, 26,000 acres known as Westover Plantation. By the end of his life, he had increased his holdings to 179,000 acres, and the islands in the James River. When approached in 1727 with a request to donate land for a city, our "reluctant city father" (as Virginius Dabney calls him) said *No*. Historians say he was trying to avoid competition for his trading post at the falls of the James. But six years later, because of pressure from Virginia's leaders, he adjusted to the idea and laid out a city.

Included in his plans was a church: St. John's Episcopal Church, after which the Church Hill neighborhood gets its name. Go to St. John's today and the tour guide of this historic property will tell you why this church was founded. William Byrd wanted to attract other people of breeding and culture to his new town, and he felt that the best way to do this was to get a respectable clergyman to come and live there. To attract such a person, Byrd felt it would be important to offer him a view of the river. Therefore he selected a site with a good view.

This motive for founding a church speaks volumes as to William Byrd's level of spirituality, especially when contrasted with Governor William Bradford of the Plymouth Colony and others to the North.

Richmond the Gateway

Byrd devoted his life to the sale of liquor, tobacco and slaves, among other commodities. He traded in rum by the thousands of gallons, and he actively promoted African slavery, turning Richmond into a major center of the slave trade.

Byrd was one of the most knowledgeable people about Virginia Indians because he traded with them far and wide. Unfortunately, one of his hottest items of trade was rum, thus opening the door to a profitable traffic in alcohol, one of the greatest curses to enter among tribal people in the history of the continent. (Compare Byrd's policies with those of Dr. John McLoughlin, the grizzled Scot who ruled trade on the West Coast at present Vancouver, Washington just west of the Cascades of the Columbia River. When he saw the harm alcohol did to Native people, he forbade the sale of all spirituous liquors to them. At one point, he purchased an entire shipload of liquor to keep it from getting into Native hands. The whole shipment was still intact at Fort Vancouver when McLoughlin retired. McLoughlin was reflecting the Christian policies of the Clapham awakening.)

Tobacco, likewise, has proven to be one of the most addictive, enslaving substances known to humankind. The tobacco crop was so central to the economy of Virginia that, at one point, it was used as currency to pay preachers in central Virginia.

Harry M. Ward, in his book *Richmond: An Illustrated History*, in the very first word of his preface, describes Richmond as "Gateway."[6] Richmond has indeed been the gateway to our country for many values, practices and influences that have predominated in our national life, which moved up the James River to the falls, and were disseminated from Richmond. I wish it could be said that these values and influences had been uniformly positive ones, but this is simply not the case.

On top of his dubious trade policies, William Byrd was a notorious womanizer. A man whose main interest was money and women was not likely to be an ideal father. Perhaps that is why his son, William Byrd III, "became an irresponsible wastrel and killed himself in 1777."[6] Despite Byrd's "breadth of mind" and "liberal thinking," he established spiritual precedents that have been anything but positive for future generations.

An Accepted Way of Life

My purpose is to show that Richmond and Williamsburg were the center of an entrenched system of domination and control that included both Church and

State, and that spread out into the commerce of the state, as it had in England. Williamsburg was, for a season, the governmental center of this system. Richmond quickly became the commercial center, based on the early influence of William Byrd and his trading post.

This is not to say that there were no Christian people among the "Knights, Gentlemen, Merchants and other Adventurers of our Citie of London"[8] who developed the "First Colony" that became known as Virginia. The First Virginia Charter does mention the "propagating of Christian Religion." However, as we trace the spirit behind those words, and discover what the first immigrants from England meant by those words, we find a great difference from the religious refugees who settled in the North.

These roots may seem like ancient history, but in the early years basic values and views were established which, once set in motion, tended to increase in impetus. The longer the spirit of domination and control prevailed, the more entrenched it became, and the idea of moving in any other direction became unthinkable.

■ ■ ■

Chapter Seven

RICHMOND DURING
THE GREAT AWAKENING

How on earth did Richmond, with its repressive, controlling ways, ever become the locale of the most famous speech of the American Revolution? —"Give me liberty or give me death!" This intriguing question is answered by local author Bob Bluford in his recent biography of Rev. Samuel Davies, the first non-Anglican preacher to be licensed in Virginia. Bob's book, *Living on the Borders of Eternity*, provides a close-up look at how the weapons of Christ work to destroy the weapons of domination and control.

Davies, before his first week on the job north of Richmond (at Polegreen, near Mechanicsville of today) appeared before Governor Gooch in Williamsburg, disarmed him with kindness and the articulation of God's word, and convinced him to grant Davies a license to preach. He then established a circuit of churches centered at the Polegreen meeting house. Here, the gospel was not only preached but lived.

The appearance of the Presbyterian on the scene was like a breath of fresh air in somebody's dungeon. Many Virginians were suffocating under the spirit of control, but didn't know what to do about it. Already, there had been 140 years moving in that direction. To quote one John Buford, in a meeting convened by William Gooch to muzzle itinerant preachers: "No itinerant has appeared in my area who has contributed to the delinquency of anyone more than the parish priest, who can at any time be found guilty of first degree assault on the human spirit. If sheer boredom were considered a deadly weapon, this priest would have been jailed long ago."[1] This bold outburst was buzzed about in the taverns of civilized Virginia— wherever authorities were unlikely to hear. Trapped in a dungeon, Virginians needed help from outside the system to get free of it.

Presbyterians Challenge the System

In those days, the Presbyterian Church was not called a denomination but a *movement*. Remember, the purpose of this movement was to oppose with the weapons of Christ, and in the name of Jesus, the spirit of domination and control. Presbyterians had been doing this for two centuries and they were good at it. They understood that the sovereignty of God does not mix with the tyranny of man. It is not hard, then, to understand why Samuel

Davies' presence in the Richmond area was so disturbing and offensive.

Until he arrived in the Richmond area, awakened Christians were tolerated only in outlying areas like the Appalachians and the Eastern shore. They were useful as buffers against Indian attack. But the moment Davies showed up in the center of civilization, alarm bells went off and the entire system geared up to oppose his presence at Polegreen.

Davies preached the true gospel so effectively that immediately Virginians were drawn from miles and miles around to hear the gospel preached in the power of the Holy Spirit. Often the people could not fit into the Polegreen meeting house so they had to conduct the service in the open air. The gospel spoke directly into the real spiritual need of people, and so Davies' reputation spread throughout the area as a real man of God. It spread, for example, into the slave population, who were just as hungry for the love of Jesus as white people were. As a result, black slaves attended church along with white Europeans, for in Christ "there is neither slave nor free."

So enamored with Davies were the slaves who attended the Polegreen meetinghouse that they invited him to their secret worship meetings in the woods at night. They treated him as a spiritual father. He, in turn, began literacy education for them as a ministry of the church. Thus, the Great Awakening spread from the Northern colonies into Virginia and the system of domination and control began to retaliate.

The clergy were bitterly resentful of this intrusion on their territory, and complained that Davies was stealing their sheep. They sent spies into his meetings to report any doctrinal irregularities they could find. Davies was harassed in various ways by the system, though the officials of the colony could find no good reason to get rid of him, and, if they had, they would have had a major popular revolt on their hands.

The adjacent Anglican priest, Rev. Patrick Henry, was at the head of the anti-Davies forces. Ironically, his sister-in-law was one of Davies' greatest supporters, and their son, Patrick, usually went to church with his mother. So it was that Patrick Henry, the future orator of the American Revolution, grew up under the preaching of Samuel Davies, and it was here that he gained all his ideas about liberty.

Samuel Davies was the best orator in Virginia, and Patrick Henry came to know what anointed preaching looked like under Davies, who became a true "father in Christ" to the young Patrick Henry. It would not be too strong to say that Samuel Davies taught Patrick Henry everything he later became famous for—ideas about liberty and powerful, persuasive speaking. We can only imagine what the conversations were like around the dinner table at the Henry house, especially whenever Uncle Patrick came to visit his brother John.

Awakened Christians Invade Virginia in Droves

Davies was only the first wave of assault on this established system. After the Presbyterians came down from the north, Dover Convention Baptists ventured in from the east. Through them God converted to Christ many of the Virginia tribes. Native people, it turned out, were hungry for the real Jesus.

Then the Methodists, who had established Methodist Societies in Suffolk and North Carolina, made their way north into central Virginia. Through them, the Holy Spirit was moving with power. For example, here is an excerpt from the diary of Thomas Rankin, a Methodist preacher from Suffolk, on June 30, 1776:

> *At four in the afternoon I preached again, from 'I set before thee an open door, and none can shut it.' I had gone through about two-thirds of my discourse, and was bringing the words home to the present—Now, when such power descended, that hundreds fell to the ground, and the house seemed to shake with the presence of God. The chapel was full of white and black, and many were without that could not get in. Look wherever we would, we saw nothing but streaming eyes, and faces bathed in tears; and heard nothing but groans and strong cries after God and the Lord Jesus Christ. My voice was drowned amidst the groans and prayers of the congregation. I then sat down in the pulpit, and both Mr. Shadford and I were so filled with the divine presence, that we could only say, This is none other than the house of God! This is the gate of heaven![2]*

And what was the result of such a move of the Spirit of God in this belated version of the Great Awakening in Virginia?

When ten Methodist preachers met for their first Conference in July 1773, the total number of men and women belonging to their societies had been 1,160.... In 1784, its membership at 14,988, Methodism had increased approximately 1,400 percent in the short span of ten years, or at a rate of about six times the increase of the American population.[3]

Richmond was openly hostile to all forms of awakened Christianity, for each of these groups brought with them ideas of freedom from the dead religious systems designed to protect domination and control by the clergy and aristocracy.

Still, winds will blow. Soon, freedom in Christ was blowing everywhere willy-nilly, and it was the talk of the town. Even aristocratic plantation owners had to deal with it.

On the other hand, having ideas about freedom was one thing; knowing what to do about them was quite another. By the 1770's, many Virginians recognized that they had inherited, and were trapped inside, a perverse system that was growing more perverse every year. The contrast between solutions bandied about can be seen in two leaders from that period, who were political rivals. I believe they became rivals because they came from very different points of view. One was Patrick Henry. The other was Thomas Jefferson.

Thomas Jefferson

Thomas Jefferson, like an increasing number of leaders, was horrified by both the perverse control of the State-sponsored Church and by African slavery. When it came to the Anglican Church system, the solution was easy: destroy it! The French, who heavily influenced Jefferson during his years in Paris, found this an easy thing to do. As soon as French revolutionaries rose to power, they confiscated Catholic Church properties and used the proceeds to fuel the Revolution.

Jefferson's antagonism to the Anglican Church was more lawful than this, and it dates from his teen years. After his father died in 1757, he lived with one of the leading Anglican clergymen of his day, the Rev. James Maury. Maury, who prided himself as a descendant of the French aristocracy, was a major voice promoting the State-controlled Church. As Fawn M. Brodie writes in her biography of Jefferson:

> *We know from a pamphlet Maury wrote attacking the Anabaptists, and from several letters his family fortuitously preserved, that he was self-righteous and bigoted, and that Patrick Henry may well have had him in mind when he wrote of the clergyman—"rapacious as a harpy" who would "snatch from the hearth of every honest*

*farmer his last hoe-cake, nay, take the last blanket
from a woman in childbirth."*

*Maury hated the Scots in Virginia colony,
calling them "raw, surly and tyrannical," and
abominated as "dupes, deceivers, and madmen"
the New Light ministers, leaders of small
evangelical sects that were threatening the
power of the state church.*[4]

Maury's hateful attitudes backfired. Thomas Jefferson
gained from this Anglican clergyman a hatred of Anglican
clergymen so deep that he devoted much of the rest of his
life to destroying their power. Brodie writes: "The
destruction of the power of the Anglican Church became
one of Jefferson's chief goals during the Revolution, and
one of his first acts as governor of Virginia and as member
of the Board of Visitors of William and Mary College in
1780 was to rout out the divines and turn the school over
to the professors of science, mathematics, and modern
languages. His distrust of clergymen as factionalists,
schismatizers, and imprisoners of the human spirit
continued to his death."[5] Today we owe to Jefferson much
of the credit for separating the black and white wires that
were constantly shorting out God's power here. But he did
not do so as a Christian.

Voltaire not Christ

Unlike most others of his time, Thomas Jefferson's
ideas about liberty were not built on a Christian

foundation, but a French one. The French were throwing away any and all scriptural ideas of freedom in preference to the tradition of Descartes, Rousseau and Voltaire. These ideas came from faith in the power of the rational mind, as opposed to the power of God's word. I will have more to say about this difference in Part Four below.

Yet Jefferson was not a thoroughgoing deist, either. He believed in God only just enough so it didn't do him any good. If he had been a deist, he would never have written the following eloquent discourse about slavery. Like many who never experienced the power of God, he more or less blamed God for allowing slavery, while not divesting himself of his own slaves. While he was President of the United States, he actually purchased eight slaves. The slaves he held at Monticello were not sold during Jefferson's lifetime. Jefferson was trapped in his head, in financial problems, and in the aristocratic system he had inherited.

As to his own inaction, he reflected philosophically in a letter to a French friend:

> *What a stupendous, what an incomprehensible machine is man! Who can endure toil, famine, stripes, imprisonment or death itself in vindication of his own liberty, and the next moment be deaf to all those motives whose power supported him thro' his trial, and inflict on his fellow men a bondage, one hour of which is fraught with more misery than ages of that which he rose in rebellion to oppose.*

*But we must await with patience the workings of
an overruling providence, and hope that that is
preparing the deliverance of these our suffering
brethren. When the measure of their tears shall be
full, when their groans shall have involved heaven
itself in darkness, doubtless a god of justice will
awaken to their distress, and by diffusing light and
liberality among their oppressors, or at length by
his exterminating thunder, manifest his attention to
the things of this world, and that they are not left to
the guidance of a blind fatality.*[6]

Neither Jefferson nor Patrick Henry (nor James
Madison, author of the Bill of Rights) could manage to
come to resolution on the slave issue, despite deep twinges
of conscience about it. The full-frontal assaults on the slave
industry would not come from Virginia, but from another
family at the top of our list of founding fathers—John
and Abigail Adams, and their son, John Quincy, Puritans
one and all.

▪ ▪ ▪

Chapter Eight

RICHMOND AND THE SECOND GREAT AWAKENING

The Puritan movement has developed a distorted reputation. This may have happened because a single event, the Salem witchcraft trials, smeared 200 years of credibility and Christian witness. That credible Christian witness continued long after the trials had come and gone.

John and Abigail Adams and their son John Quincy Adams, were Puritans. These three, who were among the most central figures in the American Revolution, demonstrate the Christian foundations on which our country was laid.

Christian Liberty

For such people, the book of Galatians was the sourcebook for convictions about Christian freedom.

These principles, underscored by Luther, Calvin and Knox, emerged to become the foundation of our most cherished American beliefs: "It is for freedom that Christ has set us free. Stand firm, then, and do not let yourselves be burdened again by a yoke of slavery" (Gal. 5:1). This verse had struck Protestants so powerfully that they were willing to suffer bitter agonies to discover and preserve it for later generations. As we have seen, some of them, for their convictions, had been sentenced to slavery, imprisonment and death by Jacobite kings and queens. Not one of them would ever have planted a cross that said, "Jacobus Rex, 1607." Not one.

But their ideas of freedom differed from French ideas, and I will have more to say about this in Part Four. Most Americans providing leadership for the Revolution were Christians, so they believed in the power of God, and they believed in ideas of freedom rooted in the Bible (as opposed to Descartes, Rousseau and Voltaire). From that biblical point of view, Christian freedom must be distinguished from license. So the book of Galatians goes on to say, "You, my brothers, were called to be free. But do not use your freedom to indulge the sinful nature; rather, serve one another in love" (Gal. 5:13).

Christ frees us *from* domination and control, but he also frees us *for* a life-style that is pleasing to God. There is a pattern to the Christian life, and without that pattern it is impossible to retain freedom. When a person is awakened by Christ, he or she is *awakened to follow that pattern*. Following the pattern is the purpose of the awakening. Awakened people want to find out what is pleasing to the Lord. He has suddenly become important to them.

The Pattern of Christ

So it is important to move to Paul's most central point in Galatians: "For in Christ Jesus...the only thing that counts is faith expressing itself through love" (Gal. 5:6). This is the pattern *into which we have been set free*, and it is the only place where true freedom may be retained: faith (in Christ) leading to love (in Christ). This pattern is consistent for all the writers of the New Testament. (See Col. 1:3-5; 1 Thess. 1:3; 1 Thess. 5:8; 2 Thess. 1:3; 1 Tim. 1:5; 1 Tim. 4:12; Tit.2:2; 2 Pet. 1:5-7; 1 Jn. 3:23.) It is this pattern that distinguishes humanistic ideas of freedom (French ideas in this case) from Christian ideas. It was on Christian ideas that our country was founded.

This pattern comes as an invasion from God into our sleeping hearts. It is the result of God's power to write His laws on our hearts—a result of God's promise, not of human effort. Minds can come along afterwards–after an awakening-miracle–and try to rationally understand what has just happened. But God's power is divine, not human, and it is tied to God's purposes, not human ones. We cannot receive God's power to use for our own purposes. In fact, we cannot use God's power at all. When it comes to the power of God, we can only surrender to it, we cannot use it.

John and Abigail Adams

Faith working through love. This is the pattern that John and Abigail Adams walked out so well, as portrayed by Irving Stone in his biographical novel, *Those Who Love*. This family, rooted in the Puritan tradition, pursued freedom for love's sake. Slavery and domination did not fit with the pattern of Christ, and so they could not abide these things. They did not pursue freedom for the sake of rationally discerned rights of man. They pursued freedom because slavery was not loving. And God is love.

The devotion of this family was passionate, not quietly rational, like Thomas Jefferson's was. In his early writing, John Adams expressed the conviction of his heart: "(Americans) have the most habitual, radical sense of liberty and the highest reverence for virtue. They are descended from a race of heroes who, placing their confidence in Providence alone, set the seas and skies, monsters and savages, tyrants and devils at defiance for the sake of religion and liberty."[1] This linking of Christian faith and freedom, this indignation against tyrants, this connection to past generations of freedom-fighters—all this expressed the feelings of a great many who had known persecution in the old country. John and Abigail taught their children accordingly.

John Quincy Adams reflected at the end of his life about his rearing, showing the roots of the family's indignation over outbreaks of domination and control:

My mother was the daughter of a Christian Clergyman and therefore bred in the faith of deliberate detestation of War.... Yet in the same Spring and Summer of 1775 she taught me to repeat daily after the Lord's prayer, before rising from bed the Ode of Collins, on the patriot warriors who fell in the War to subdue the Jacobite rebellion of 1745.[2]

A Contagion of Liberty

We have seen that the roots of Virginia go back to England. So do the roots of New England, and they were very different roots from the South. The American Civil War was rooted in the civil wars of the old country. They were rooted in two entirely different visions of what Christ came to do. One group thought that Christ came to establish a hierarchical system of privilege and control. The other group thought that Christ came to abolish all such systems, and to assert Himself as the only true Lord. The latter group prevailed in this country, and we can all be very, very thankful that they did. Also – it is necessary to say – both groups could not be right. One was right and the other was wrong.

Abigail Adams was nearly as strong an influence on the American Revolution as her husband and son. It was Abigail who most ardently expressed Christian outrage toward the plight of black slaves, a slave industry that had invaded even Boston and the precincts of the Pilgrims:

> *I wish most sincerely that there was not a slave in the province. It always seemed a most iniquitous scheme to me—to fight ourselves for what we are daily robbing and plundering from those who have as good a right to freedom as we have.*

Or again:

> *I have sometimes been ready to think that the passion for liberty cannot be equally strong in the breasts of those who have been accustomed to deprive their fellow-creatures of theirs. Of this I am certain, that it is not founded upon that generous and Christian principle of doing to others as we would that others should do unto us.*[3]

Those who fought for freedom at Bunker Hill, who braved the dangers of open war and, who lost children or parents in the war for freedom, sometimes bitterly resented leaders from the South for their duplicity on the slave issue. To be sure, there could always be found politicians, preachers and businessmen in the North who waffled as much as any Southerner. But slavery was being exterminated in the North, state by state, between 1777 and 1804 through what one historian called "the contagion of Liberty." Increasingly, leaders who had fought for freedom in the North became impatient with Southern foot-dragging with regard to slavery, which they believed was offensive to Christ, and a blight on our most cherished principles.

John Quincy Adams

For example, in 1845, John Quincy Adams reflected in his diary about a memorial celebration at the granite monument at Bunker Hill, and a dinner following at Fanueil Hall, to honor the memory of those who had fought for freedom during the American Revolution. These events were attended by two Southerners, John Tyler and Daniel Webster, with his black slave holding an umbrella over his head. JQA wrote in his diary: "Daniel Webster is a heartless traitor to the cause of human freedom; John Tyler is a slave-monger. What have these to do with the Quincy granite pyramid on the brow of Bunker Hill? What have these to do with a dinner in Faneuil Hall, but to swill like swine, and grunt about the rights of man? I stayed home and visited my seedling trees."[4]

And again, in 1820, Adams expressed in his journal, "Oh, if but one man could arise with a genius capable of comprehending, a heart capable of supporting, and an utterance capable of communicating those eternal truths that belong to this question, to lay bare in all its nakedness that outrage upon the goodness of God, human slavery, now is the time, and this is the occasion, upon which such a man would perform the duties of an angel upon earth."[5]

If there was any such angel, it was JQA himself, who was the two-edged sword-tip that forced the issue again and again in Congress, and also in the Supreme Court by defending the slaves of the ship, *Amistad*. JQA became the only president in history to return to the Senate after his presidency, which he did to carry on the fight against slavery.

After him, as we have seen, the new generation of Christians that grew up from the Finney revivals, with Theodore Dwight Weld and Lewis Tappan at their head, developed abolitionist societies that kept on forcing the issue throughout the country–all resulting from the Second Great Awakening–and almost entirely in the North. (Perhaps it is significant that Kentucky, the starting point for the Second Great Awakening, though it was considered a Southern state, refused to join the Secession movement, and was not part of the Confederacy.)

The slave issue forced out into the open underlying differences of world-view that had to be confronted sooner or later, issues that required conflict in this country, just as they had done in Scotland and in England. At heart was the issue of what kind of person God is, what kind of Kingdom Jesus brings, and what God wants of us in following the first and second commandments, the love commandments. These were not abstruse debates about the meaning of "slavery" in Genesis and Exodus. They got down to the most basic issues of what it means to be a Christian and what kind of God we follow.

Richmond and Gabriel's Insurrection

Virginia was caught between this impassioned pursuit of Christian liberty, and the hard-edged system of domination and control that had grown up in the Deep

South. The "contagion of liberty" had dripped down from the North as though through sheer gravitational pull, to infect men like James Madison, George Washington, Patrick Henry and Thomas Jefferson, plantation owners, one and all. Virginia had been genuinely struggling with the principles of liberty, trying to emerge from rank duplicity on the slavery issue, but having a very difficult time of it.

Then, in 1799, came Gabriel's insurrection, in the very year that the Second Great Awakening began in Logan County, Kentucky. Gabriel was Thomas Prosser's most trusted slave. The Prosser plantation was located near Brook Road on the north side of Richmond, south of the Crump plantation. Gabriel succeeded in developing a network of slave insurrectionists from Charlottesville to the Tidewater area. The killing was to begin with the Prosser family and spread throughout the state. The first blow would fall on Saturday night, August 30.

Slaves had amassed an arsenal of mostly hand-made weapons. The plan was to set fire to the wooden buildings along Richmond's waterfront at Rocketts. The white people of Richmond would rush en masse from Shockoe Hill and Church Hill down to the river to put out the flames. Thousands of slaves would then enter the city from the north and take over the city. They would kill the citizens of Richmond returning from fire-fighting, and hopefully capture Governor James Monroe.

The plot failed partly due to an unusual storm that rose up in the middle of the fateful night, causing the streams to flood, and hindering communications among the insurrectionists. But the rebellion was not without effect on the spirit of people in Richmond. It created fear which was to hang over the city, hardening people on the issue of slavery. These fears seemed to center in Richmond, which was the source of insurrection rumors again in 1808, 1809 and 1813. Dabney summarizes:

> *All this unrest among the slaves, especially that evidenced in Gabriel's attempted insurrection, caused a marked lessening of efforts by the whites to abolish chattel servitude. Such efforts had been actively pursued in the years following the Revolution, albeit without tangible results. But after 1800 the trend was the other way, and the Virginia Abolition Society ceased to function, as did all other such societies in the South. Not only so, but Virginia passed a law in 1806 providing that any slave who was freed had to leave the state within twelve months.* [6]

Richmond's Churches

Richmond chuches were not exempt from the spirit of domination and control. Following the Second Great Awakening, Richmond tardily opened its gates to non-Anglican churches. Ward summarizes: "From its very slow start, Richmond was developing into a city of churches, tallying 35 Christian and three Jewish houses of worship by 1860."

Almost from the start, however, these churches adapted the gospel to fit into the prevailing spirit of the city. Even denominations that had been birthed during awakenings of Christian liberty succumbed to that spirit when they moved into Richmond. The love, liberty and equality so beautifully demonstrated in the ministry of Samuel Davies had to take a back seat to the sheer inertia of a city that had been walking in domination and control for two centuries.

One such church, quoted by Ward, more or less seems to represent the attitude of church people throughout the city: "It was quite impossible for the pastor, with a large white congregation under his care, to pay much attention to the necessities of the colored portion of his flock." Ward goes on to comment, "What was not mentioned was the increased emphasis on caste (racism), as Southerners were becoming hard pressed to justify the institution of slavery."[7]

Typical of that caste system was an ordinance passed in Richmond: "Negroes shall not at any time stand on a side-walk to the inconvenience of persons passing by. A Negro meeting or overtaking, or being overtaken by a white person on a side-walk, shall pass on the outside; and if it be necessary to enable such white person to pass, shall immediately get off the side-walk."[8]

The Slave Market

During this period Richmond was the center of a very prosperous slave trade. Slaves were transported by ship to

Ancarrow's landing and marched to Lumpkin's jail in Shockoe Bottom. These slave processions were done under cover of darkness at night, so as not to offend those with sensitive consciences. The slave trail on the south side of the river is well marked today at James River Park on the far east end of Maury Street. The trade was carried on in the area bounded by Franklin street, Broad street, 15th and 17th streets. Between 20 and 50 slaves were auctioned daily. Each slave was made to stand naked before the potential buyers, so that no blemishes could be covered up by clothing.

The Fear of Losing Control

All this occurred at the very time God was moving so dramatically around the world to rid His world of slavery. These efforts would continue to grow, but in Richmond, fear prevented them from entering the city. The South, as a whole, closed itself off from what God was speaking elsewhere. Richmond was trying to cling in its dying gasp to a system of domination and control that it still identified as perfectly Christian.

The result? An increasing division between the North, where Revival fires were provoking the proliferation of Abolitionist Societies—and the South, where self-protection ruled the day. William Lee Miller interprets this phenomenon:

> *There were…in the case of the slave industry,*
> *unique elements of fear. What would happen if*

the slaves were freed? Millions of systematically
mistreated people would suddenly be out from
under the social control that slavery provided.[9]

The Revival of 1857-1859

Yet God had mercy on the South, for the next great wave of spiritual awakening began in the South, primarily among African American slaves, as I have shown.

In Richmond, however, it is difficult to see the results of the movement. It didn't make enough of a splash to appear in the histories of Richmond. Samuel Prime, the main chronicler of the movement, does mention Richmond as having been touched by the movement—but no details. Just an honorable mention at the end of the book.

What surely hindered Richmond was, again, fear. True, many in Richmond were trying to counsel reconciliation, and there was much sympathy for slaves. But, in contrast to news articles about prayer meetings in other cities, this is what appeared in the *Enquirer* on Dec. 6, 1859, in the wake of the most recent attempted slave insurrection (as it was perceived to be):

(John Brown's execution) may as effectually rally
the conservatives, as it assuredly will the fanatics
(with their) demoniac spirit that prevails among
Northern men–not all–God forbid! But those
whose morbid appetites for blood have been
whetted by the stimulating influences of the
prayer and saint-like doctrines preached by the

Beechers and Cheevers and other such presumptuous servants of God.

The article went on to say that any slave insurgency inspired by abolitionists in Virginia would be met "with ropes for which South Carolina grows the cotton, and Kentucky the hemp."[10]

Ironically, it was the news from Charleston—the fall of Fort Sumpter and the conscription of an army by President Lincoln against Southern secessionists—that forced the decision for Virginia to secede from the Union. This decision made Richmond what Harry M. Ward calls "a city under siege, a city of refuge."[11] In spite of the contagion of liberty dripping down from the north, the capitol of Virginia became *a city of refuge* from that contagion.

■ ■ ■

Chapter Nine

THE CIVIL WAR

In the aftermath of the Second Great Awakening, an amazing thing happened. Britain repented of the slave trade. The English turned around exactly 180 degrees and walked in the opposite direction: from encouraging the most cruel form of slavery ever practiced—to enforcing its abolition throughout the world. They didn't just stop doing it. They decided to stop everyone else from doing it as well. The very weapons that had initiated this nefarious trade were now used to commandeer slave ships, arrest slavers and free slaves world-wide. England forced its Christian morality on everyone. Britain used its vast naval superiority to abolish slavery on the high seas world-wide, no matter who was practicing it. From 1833 on, England spent huge sums blockading the African coast to stamp out the slave trade.

Call it repentance.

Nowhere in history do we have a clearer illustration of what can happen when Jesus awakens the hearts of a few Christians who move into government and change the direction of a nation—and the world.

The Gateway Becomes the City of Refuge

A different thing happened in this country. In the North, a similar Christian indignation was seizing the populace, but, as we have seen, the Deep South was gripped by fear and threatening to secede from the Union.

Virginia was caught between the North and the South, profoundly conflicted. Richmond, in 1860, was overwhelmingly opposed to secession as was Virginia. At the Virginia Convention in Richmond that year, delegates voted 88 to 45 against secession.

But when President Lincoln put muscle to the rhetoric of preserving the Union–asking Virginia to help him raise a volunteer army to put down secessionist rebellion in the Deep South, sentiment shifted. The following day, April 16, 1861, the Convention reversed position, voting to secede. All three Richmond delegates voted with the majority.

On April 22nd, Robert E. Lee, who had just declined an offer to command the Northern armies, moved to Richmond to raise a Confederate army. "Although strongly opposed to secession prior to Lincoln's appeal for Virginia troops, Lee, who owned not a single slave, gave up stately Arlington and impoverished himself and his family to cast his lot with the land of his birth. He recognized from the first that it was a well-nigh hopeless cause."[1]

A week later Jefferson Davis was invited from Montgomery, Alabama, to head the Confederate government. Confederate leaders decided to make Richmond the capital because of the Tredegar Iron works, the excellent hotels, and the city's history of political leadership.

Richmond, the Gateway thus became Richmond, the City of Refuge—a last bastion of protection for a way of life that was being snuffed out everywhere else in the world. Very quickly, a chain of seventeen forts was erected to protect the city from the outside world.

My theme in this book is that Jesus, the King, was and is opposed to all forms of domination and control. I am trying to show that the abolition of slavery, like the abolition of aristocratic tyranny, was a product of successive waves of spiritual awakening—Christian spiritual movements that forced all nations to find ways of governing themselves other than by domination and control. The way of Christ is the way of love and humility, and Christian governments were trying to discover how to work this out in public and political ways—not just private ways. Christ is Lord of all, not just of our private lives, but also of public policies. He hates corporate sin just as much as private sin.

Abraham Lincoln

If my basic theme is correct, no one found himself more perfectly a target of God's severe mercy than the President of the United States at that critical moment of our history, the Civil War years.

Abraham Lincoln was an unlikely candidate to be a servant of God's higher purposes. According to William Herndon, Lincoln's law partner, Lincoln was not even a Christian. Herndon describes him as a believer in "natural religion," a sort of deist, perhaps. Certainly, there is no evidence that Abe Lincoln was raised a Christian, not by any stretch of the imagination.

Yet all the indications are that the burden of the Presidency forced him to give his life to Christ and depend on God as he undertook the heavy responsibility of the Presidency. The office of the Presidency during the Civil War became Lincoln's opportunity to learn how to draw near to God and trust His power over nations:

General James F. Rusling gives a most interesting account of a call he and General Daniel E. Sickles made upon him after the battle of Gettysburg. During the conversation General Sickles asked if the President and the Cabinet had not been anxious about the battle? Mr. Lincoln replied that the Cabinet had, but he had not; and he then went on to make a confession that in the very pinch and stress of the Gettysburg campaign he had gone to the Almighty in secret prayer. He said he told the Lord

this was his country, and the war was his war, but
that we could not stand another Fredericksburg or
Chancellorsville; and that he then and there made a
solemn vow with his Maker that if he would stand by
us at Gettysburg, he would stand by him, and then
he added: "And he did, *and I* will!" *He said that*
after he had prayed, he could not explain how it was,
but a sweet comfort had crept into his soul that God
Almighty had taken the whole business there into his
hands, and we were bound to win at Gettysburg.[2]

Most of the battles of the Civil War had gone against Lincoln's forces up to that point through the sheer dithering and incompetence of Union generals. But at Gettysburg, through the bravery of an abolitionist Christian with little or no military training—Joshua Chamberlain—the fortunes of the Union army turned sharply upwards in the battle for Little Round Top. It was the day the tide of war turned. (By the way, according to my son, who is completing his doctoral work in this area, the film "Gettysburg" is very accurate in its portrayal of all persons and events connected with the battle.)

The Second Inaugural

Lincoln's heart became so burdened with God's moral demands with regard to slavery that they dominated his second inaugural speech. Facing the fact that both sides in the Civil War drew upon the Bible to justify their side of it, toward the end of the war he observed:

Both read the same Bible and pray to the same God, and each invokes his aid against the other. It may seem strange that any man should dare to ask a just God's assistance in wringing their bread from the sweat of other men's faces, but let us judge not that we be not judged. The prayers of both could not be answered. That of neither has been answered fully. The Almighty has his own purposes. "Woe unto the world because of offences, for it must needs be that offences come; but woe to the man by whom the offence cometh." If we shall suppose that American slavery is one of these offences, which in the providence of God must needs come, but which, having continued through his appointed time, he now wills to remove, and that he gives to both North and South this terrible war as the woe due to those by whom the offence came, shall we discern therein any departure from those divine attributes which the believers in a living God always ascribe to him? Fondly do we hope, fervently do we pray, that this mighty scourge of war may soon pass away. Yet, if God wills that it shall continue until all the wealth piled by the bondman's two hundred and fifty years of unrequited toil shall be sunk, and until every drop of blood drawn with the lash shall be paid with another drawn with the sword; as was said three thousand years ago, so it still must be said, "The judgments of the Lord are true and righteous altogether."[3]

Many who spoke with Lincoln during his last years remarked that, underneath the jocularity of his manner, there lay a deep sadness, a burdensomeness of duty that engulfed him and all his actions. Lincoln was seized not only with God's compassion for slaves, but also with God's compassion for the Deep South. That compassion drew him to visit Richmond very soon after the city surrendered to Union forces.

Fear Hath Torment

On the other side, Richmonders had been horrified to see the fortunes of war turn against them. Huge streams of wounded soldiers had flowed into the city to be treated at the city's hospitals, probably the best hospitals in the country. The largest of these was located at Chimborazo Park. Increasingly, Richmond fell under a paranoia toward Lincoln and the North, leading to tragic consequences.

Thus, at the end of the war, Richmond was in no position to appreciate Lincoln's compassion, nor the burden under which the President labored. By the end of the war, Richmond had demonized the President to such a degree that fear-talk had turned to hate-mongering against the President. Northern troops were seen as blue-coated demons who would rape the women, kill the city fathers and abscond with all the hard-won resources they had labored for.

The greatest disaster in Richmond's history up to then had been the theater fire at the Richmond Theater in 1811, where hundreds of people had trampled each other to death in their panic. By the end of the War, all Richmond was a theater; panicky Richmonders, overwhelmed with deceptive fear, decided that extreme measures were required as Northern troops entered their city.

Though Mayor Mayo warned of the danger of torching the stocks of tobacco, General Richard S. Ewell carried out the agreed-upon act to prevent their falling to the enemy. Soon after the fire was lit, a strong wind blew in from the south, fanning the flames into other buildings. The fire gutted most of the center of the city, 900 buildings in all.

Ironically, when the Union Army did enter the city, the feared rampaging of Union soldiers did not materialize. Virginius Dabney summarizes:

The Union commander ordered all Northern troops, white and black, to behave with utmost correctness and protect citizens and property. These orders were carried out. There was universal praise for the conduct of the Union troops. Thousands of black soldiers were billeted at Camp Lee and strict discipline was maintained. Mrs. Robert E. Lee remained in her scorched house and told her husband later, "It is impossible to describe the kind attentions of the Union soldiers."

On April 4, President Lincoln appeared suddenly in Richmond after sailing upriver from City Point.[4]

Lincoln was trying to reassure the capital of the Confederacy that he had no evil intentions toward any Southerner, and would work to rebuild the South. Richmond stood a better fate by Lincoln than by Jefferson Davis, the City Council and the Virginia General Assembly, who a few days before, had voted to burn the city rather than let it fall into enemy hands. Plans had been made to blow up the Capital. But the Confederate leaders had all fled the city before their plans had been carried out.

Then came the return of the great, but defeated, war hero, Robert E. Lee.

Six days went by, and there was no direct word from Lee. Then all at once a forlorn caravan appeared in the drenching rain on the pontoon bridge across the James. The weary and worn commander of the Army of Northern Virginia was riding his famous war horse Traveller, his hat and clothing were soaked, and several officers who accompanied him were equally waterlogged....

Arrival of the group at the bridge was noted at once and crowds gathered quickly. Cheers rang out and hats were thrown into the air when Lee hove into view. Union soldiers joined heartily in the tribute of respect to this man who had held them at bay for four years against overwhelming odds. There were tears from those who saw the grizzled warrior as the symbol of the fallen

Confederacy. He lifted his head time and again in acknowledgement of the tributes. Finally he arrived at his residence, 707 E. Franklin Street, where a throng awaited him. These citizens of Richmond, young and old, hoped to take his hand or touch his uniform. Some were sobbing. Lee himself was deeply moved and on the verge of losing his self-control. He grasped as many hands as he could, then made his way through the gate and up the steps. Bowing to the crowd, he entered the house and closed the door.

It was a sad hour for the onetime capital of the Confederacy, but further calamities lay ahead. On April 15, the day that Lee returned from Appomatox, news of President Lincoln's assassination reached the city. It was the ultimate disaster—for Richmond, Virginia and the South…. The wise and tolerant policies enunciated by President Lincoln would now be superseded by those of the vengeful Northern radicals.[5]

Today, President Lincoln is still vilified in Richmond. To quote a recent issue of Richmond Magazine: "Only in Richmond could erecting a statue of Honest Abe cause controversy."[6]

My conviction, though, is that Lincoln was not to blame for the Civil War and the destruction of Richmond.

Lincoln was under a burden from God that he could not escape. He was pursuing God's wish for a nation that He wanted to hold up as a beacon of liberty and love.

William Tecumseh Sherman

Before I end this section, one more thing must be said, though it does not impinge directly on Richmond's history. It affected Richmond indirectly by increasing the climate of fear already present here, and it complicates the healing of our country to this day.

In May of 1864, Ulysses S. Grant sent William Tecumseh Sherman on his Atlanta campaign, a scorched-earth and highly destructive march that cut the South in two and destroyed everything in its path, including the city of Atlanta. Sherman took warfare to a new level of destructiveness, believing that it was necessary to crush the war spirit in the opponent to achieve ultimate peace. Sherman's march was aimed not only at destroying the South's infrastructure, but crushing the spirit of the Old South. He believed that this was necessary to bring a fractious and rebellious people to their knees, or there would never be peace. He expressed his thoughts in perhaps the most famous letter of the Civil War era, his letter to the Atlanta city council expressing why he was about to torch their city (available at www.rjgeib.com/thoughts/sherman/sherman-to-burn-atlanta.html).

After the war, Sherman took this philosophy out West and used it against the plains tribes—Comanches, Kiowas,

Cheyennes and Sioux. He is responsible for many of the most destructive and crushing massacres of Western history, again believing that Native people must have the war spirit crushed out of them. It was on the back of Sherman's military philosophy that our country attained the geographical unity that we now enjoy. But at what cost!

Those who had the "war spirit" crushed out of them feel the cost of unity to this day, whereas those who rode on the back of Sherman's victories tend to think, "Why don't they just get over it?" This lingering resentment remains today both in the South and the Indian reservations of the West. But there is more.

Even Sherman, one of the most ruthless military commanders of his time, could not stomach the governmental policies that Washington imposed on the people he had conquered. These policies amounted to "kicking a man when he is down." Dee Brown's excellent history, *Bury My Heart at Wounded Knee*, testifies to the fact that in later years, Sherman took up cause against Washington politicians to defend the Plains tribes he himself had forced onto reservations.

This should tell us something about ourselves as a nation. Once we had attained unity through force of arms, and had achieved a centralized government, we were far from gracious toward the peoples we had subdued in the process. In fact, we turned the knife in the wound, and that knife remains "turned" to this day. The vindictive and incompetent leaders we elected following Abraham

Lincoln have greatly complicated the possibility of healing during succeeding generations. There are still many unhealed, twisted wounds that remain both in the Old South and in the West on Indian reservations. But I believe God wants to bring just such healing, and that this healing is necessary to pave the way for a national spiritual awakening.

■ ■ ■

Chapter Ten

THE JIM CROW ERA

We have seen how, during the Azusa Street Revival, God used a black man, William Seymour, to usher in an extraordinary awakening of love in the heart of Los Angeles, the most polyglot city in America. For a few brief years, love prevailed in that community, which reflected the will of the Holy Spirit. Again, my conviction is that God was expressing Himself, personally making a statement by His choice of leaders. I believe that in the spiritual awakenings of our history, God most clearly expressed His heart.

Here in Richmond, however, we were still dealing with a spirit of domination and control. You cannot get rid of a spirit by means of a political change or a military victory alone. When the government changes, that spirit simply finds another way to express itself. The spirit of domination and control found many ways of expressing itself during the decades following the Civil War. First on the list was a social system called Jim Crow.

In Richmond, Jim Crow restrictions–a product of white supremacy and the spirit of domination and control–can be traced back to the Reconstruction years, 1865-1870.

> *At first blacks only rode on the outside of streetcars; then white balls were attached to coaches reserved for whites only. Blacks were intimidated from patronizing the better hotels and restaurants and hence, established their own. Theaters also were segregated with seating for blacks in the galleries.*[1]

Challenging Jim Crow

To catch a glimpse of this system during the pre-Martin Luther King days, I sought an interview with Dr. Robert Taylor, a personal friend, and one of the "elders" of Richmond during those times. He recalled the years of his childhood, when he moved from Hanover County into Richmond.

> *In Hanover County (as a boy), we could go to the stores and buy and eat in the stores and we always felt welcomed and loved. As I grew older and moved to Richmond, I became sensitive of the differences in this city. I would go with my*

brother to the store and he would say, "No, Robert, we can't go in there." Then we would get on the bus, and we would go to sit down and he would say, "No, Robert, we can't sit there. We have to go to the back."

(Later as a minister,) I felt that now, becoming a grown person, it gave me an attitude toward segregation and I felt that I would have as much responsibility of doing something about segregation as anyone.

Now there were some students from Virginia Union who went to (Thalhimer's)...and they were asked to leave and they didn't leave, and they were arrested.... The pastors came together to discuss the situation. Mr. Thalhimer was there and they asked us as black preachers to advise those black students not to come to their store. ...And we said, "No." I said to Mr. Thalhimer, "Since you're not willing to integrate your store, I am giving you my Thalhimer's card," and I put my card on his knee and said, "When you integrate your store, then I'll come and pick up my card." And he kept it.

One Friday, I was coming back from Fredericksburg. My wife said, "Taylor, Thalhimer has integrated his store!"

I said, "You mean it? He has?"

"Yes. His store is integrated."

"I'm going to Thalhimer's tomorrow."

Saturday morning came, and I went to Thalhimers....

The lady in the office buzzed Mr. Thalhimer... I went up to his office.

He gathered everybody on his level of the store and he stood there and gave one of the finest speeches I have ever heard. He said, "If I had been in your place, I'd have done the same thing." And he got my credit card and gave it back to me.[2]

To my mind, the significance of this story has to do with the search for Christian integrity. For hundreds of years, the gospel of Christ in Richmond had been fit into the agenda of a spirit of domination and control. When Christians give in to that spirit, which is foreign to Christ, it destroys the integrity of the Church, which is called to represent Christ.

In Richmond, there has been a profound confusion about the meaning of the gospel. The name of Jesus is pasted on the outside of systems that are essentially antichristian. We use the name of Christ to give legitimacy to our systems—like the "Jesus of Lubeck" sign pasted on the outside of the first slave ship.

In this story, certain pastors and business leaders wanted Dr. Taylor to once again legitimize the systems of domination and control that had set themselves up in

Richmond. In the name of Christ, he refused. In my mind, this was a profoundly Christian act, and it deserves to be honored as such. The issue was not whether blacks should find acceptance in white culture and white society. The real issue was whether Christians will stand up and confront the spirit of domination and control that has been allowed to prevail in this city for so many centuries.

Walter Plecker

During my acquaintance with Native tribes in Virginia, I discovered how they have felt about Richmond and its influence on their lives. Their experience in the twentieth century again reflects, not the Spirit of Christ, but the spirit of domination and control. I was a visitor to several meetings of the Council on Indian Affairs several years ago. It didn't take long to discover the number one hurt that we whites have inflicted on Virginia Natives: the attempt by white Virginians to obliterate their identity as the First Nations on this continent.

This happened in Richmond under the leadership of Walter Plecker, Registrar of the Bureau of Vital Statistics.

A physician born just before the Civil War, Plecker embraced the now-discredited eugenics movement as a scientific rationale for preserving Caucasian racial purity. He saw only two races, Caucasian and non-Caucasian, and staunchly opposed their "amalgamation."

After helping win passage in 1924 of a strict race classification and anti-miscegenation law

*called the Racial Integrity Act, Plecker engaged
in a zealous campaign to prevent what he
considered "destruction of the white or higher
civilization."*

*When he perceived Indians as threats to
enforcing the color line, he used the tools of
his office to endeavor to crush them and deny
their existence.*

*Many Western tribes experienced government
neglect during the 20th century, but the Virginia
story was different: The Indians were consciously
targeted for mistreatment.*

*Plecker changed racial labels on vital records
to classify Indians as "colored," investigated the
pedigrees of racially "suspect" citizens, and
provided information to block or annul
interracial marriages with whites. He testified
against Indians who challenged the law.*

*Virginia's Indians refused to die out, although
untold numbers moved away or assumed a
low profile.*[3]

Eugenics was an attempt, growing out of evolutionary
theory and genetics research, to improve the human race
through controlled breeding, assuring that humans with
good genes would advance the human race to its ultimate
destiny. Adolf Hitler, a great believer in eugenics, saw
Walter Plecker as a positive example of what could be done
to advance the cause of white (Aryan) supremacy.

George Allen, as Governor of Virginia, formally apologized for the many years of mistreatment of Native Virginians during the days of Walter Plecker. Still, what we are concerned about as Christians is the witness of the Church and the redemptive message of Christ during all those years. What were Christians doing to alleviate this situation? Was a heart of prayer changing anything in Richmond during the days of Jim Crow restrictions and Walter Plecker experiments in eugenics?

The Grief in the Heart of God

Perhaps here, I could insert a personal note as an intercessor. It is, in part, this experience that impassions my own writing of this book. Soon after God brought me to Richmond in 1985, He drew me up to the Library of Congress in 1986 to research the beginnings of white-Native relations in this country. Honestly, I wanted to see what had happened to the passion of my forefathers, the Pilgrims, to bring the gospel to Native people.

What I discovered in my research took my breath away. I have shared briefly in my book, *The Church at Richmond*, how God had been speaking to Native prophets about Jesus before any white people came among them. I saw the heart of God to bring Native people to Jesus, so they could know His love. I saw how God had paved the way for us white Christians to do our job, witnessing to the love of Jesus among them.

But then I saw why we had failed in this, so that, by today, only 6% of Native people have actually embraced the gospel. I read with bewilderment how white people purposely enslaved them to alcohol during the fur trade years, then defrauded them of their lands, broke every treaty we ever made with them, abused their women, shoved them off into a corner of our emerging country, and finally took their children away from them, placing them in Indian boarding schools to make them adopt our culture.

And where was the Church in all this naked abuse of power? Right in the middle of it, going along with it and often leading it.

One particular Native American Christian from the Pacific Northwest became, for me, a representative of the whole. Spokan Garry was the first Native preacher in the Pacific Northwest. A great Revival among Native people in 1828 can be traced to his preaching among the tribes there. But I traced his story beyond those years into the 1860's and '70's. I read how the first Presbyterians and Anglicans led the way in defrauding Spokan Garry (a fellow believer) of his lands. They threw him off his property and stood by while he and his people were disgraced and debauched. I could not believe how this could be the witness of the Church of Jesus Christ. "How could this happen, Lord?" I asked again and again.

One day, I was in prayer. People had gathered around me to pray for my back which was in pain. Suddenly, a word came forth: "This back condition you have is a result of ancestral sin. Someone in your lineage, apparently, has committed sin against Native Americans, and has brought this curse. You need to ask God to forgive this sin and heal it."

All this was news to me. I had no idea of who might have committed such sin. But I wanted to be obedient to the word, if it was based on truth. When I opened my mouth to ask God's forgiveness, God, without warning, downloaded such grief and pain into my heart that I wept bitterly for half an hour without even knowing what I was crying about. After that, I would break out weeping whenever I would think about Native people, or at times when I would be in their presence. It was then that my research about Spokan Garry went from my head to my heart (though this research did not relate to my ancestry, as far as I know).

Getting In Touch With God's Loving Heart

This is what I believe was happening here: I was getting in touch with God's heart, His heart of love for all people—especially the people we have abused when we were seized by the spirit of domination and control. I learned this important lesson as an intercessor: There is great grief in God's heart, more than we can possibly bear to experience. Much of that grief has been caused by us. The worst of it has happened when we have pasted the name of Jesus on the outside of our systems of domination and control.

I believe I was getting in touch with the same God that George Fox and the early Quakers heard from; the same God who fired the hearts of early Moravians with compassion for slaves; the same God who impassioned William Wilberforce and Theodore Dwight Weld to end slavery; the same God who raised up Dr. Martin Luther King, Jr. to stand against Jim Crow racism.

What I have become aware of so keenly, deeply and incessantly is that all of us, whether we like it or not, and whether we realize it or not, are going to have to answer to Jesus for what we did in His name. In the end, we will realize what King David voiced 3,000 years ago: "Against Thee, and Thee only have I sinned."

■ ■ ■

Part Three

THE PROMISE
OF SPIRITUAL
AWAKENING
FOR RICHMOND

Chapter Eleven

SURRENDERING CONTROL TO GOD

Before I convey the promises I believe God has given me for Richmond, which relate to Richmond's future, let me try to summarize what I believe is the relevance of this "spiritual mapping" of Richmond's past. Why, for example, would a city that has a long history of domination and control (and the fear of losing control) have difficulty entering into a spiritual awakening? The answer has to do with the nature of spiritual awakenings and the power of God.

We open our lives to God's power by surrendering our lives to Jesus. God's power is not something we "use." It is something we surrender to. It overtakes us. It flows through surrendered, yielded people. We do not get it. It gets us.

What!? Give Up Control of My Life to Someone Else?

Most of us would be leery of turning over our lives to someone besides ourselves. We want to stay in control of our lives. Giving up personal control and personal choice seems like suicide to most Americans. However, when we become Christians, it is usually because we realize that Jesus is worthy of our trust and He can make our lives turn out better than we could do for ourselves. Whether we realize it or not, we are all ensconced in a good deal of self-deception—and Jesus is not! He sees more clearly than we do, even into our own hearts. His will for us is entirely good and loving. He who knows us best loves us most.

Many people do not believe this because of the bad witness of churches that have been overtaken by a spirit of domination and control—making them very hurtful. Many people have gained from this a false impression about Jesus, that He is hurtful and controlling. Some groups of people have experienced much harm through churches; they will have to re-discover Jesus in some fresh way if they will surrender their lives to Him.

We find out the truth about Jesus by going back to the cross of Christ—His death, which proclaims the love of God for us. "For God so loved the world that he gave his only begotten Son, that whosoever should believe in him will not perish, but have everlasting life" (Jn. 3:16). Mel Gibson's film, *The Passion of the Christ*, is helping many people reconnect with this "dying love."

God responded to Jesus' total and joyful surrender to the Father's will by raising Him to life, causing Him to ascend to a place of eternal rulership "at His right hand," and pouring out the Holy Spirit to draw people to Jesus. Those who recognize these historic facts are then invited to look to Jesus as a model of life, for He left us an example, that we should follow in His steps (see 1 Pet. 2:21). As we comprehend the love of God, we, through Christ, have the right to become sons and daughters of God through Jesus. The Holy Spirit will then re-create us after His image. We are challenged to lay down our lives as did Jesus...

> *who, being in very nature God,*
> *did not consider equality with God something*
> *to be grasped,*
> *but made himself nothing,*
> *taking the very nature of a servant,*
> *being made in human likeness.*
> *And being found in appearance as a man,*
> *he humbled himself*
> *and became obedient unto death—*
> *even death on a cross.*
> *Therefore God exalted him to the highest place*
> *and gave him the name that is above every name,*
> *that at the name of Jesus every knee should bow,*
> *in heaven and on earth and under the earth,*
> *and every tongue confess that Jesus Christ is Lord,*
> *to the glory of God the Father. (Phil. 2:5-11)*

Now we recognize that Jesus is "the Christ." He is the Coming King, the One who deserves, by His loving and gentle way, and by His sacrifice on the cross, to be Lord of all. Therefore, He deserves to be Lord *of us*. Therefore, He is worthy of the surrender of our lives to Him. The moment we see who Jesus is, there is only one appropriate response: surrender. That implies that we must give up our urge to dominate and control.

Burning Our Cities

Though such a decision may seem like suicide at first, there are several ways that this decision of surrender makes sense, especially to those who have experienced the hard realities of life. From the history of Richmond we learn this valuable lesson: that people who refuse to surrender control are likely to burn down their own city. We can become deceived by the fear of losing control. Fear becomes a life style leading to deep deception. Many of us are living that life style every day of our lives. "Fear hath torment." The only real security comes from surrendering our lives to God.

Surrender to God delivers us from fear, anxiety and much of the stress that is today's number one killer. And if we are going to surrender our lives to someone, Jesus alone is worthy of this kind of faith. All others are "thieves and robbers." All others will betray our confidence sooner or later.

A Life of Frustration

People who try to stay in control are doomed to a life of frustration. They do not know how to live their lives in harmony with God. Henry VIII took control and dominated the Church with dungeon and sword. By means of intimidation, he was trying to manipulate his personal destiny so that he could have a male heir.

In the end, however, the most important heir from Henry's loins was a woman: Elizabeth I. He married six wives trying to achieve a male heir. This attempt to manipulate his destiny brought misery to thousands, who were forced to flee across the ocean to obtain relief from the persecution of Henry and his heirs. This is where domination and control usually ends. We don't often gain the things we are striving for. We just create misery—often to our own loved ones.

The surrendered life may not seem as secure as the other kind. But it ends up in a better place, and it avoids many of the frustrations of trying to achieve things through manipulation.

While there have been seasons when the Church has manifested a spirit of domination and control because people with unsurrendered lives (like Henry VIII) have wormed their way into key leadership positions in the Church, these seasons are not to be seen as normal. I have presented these seasons as hostile take-overs of the Church. Christ does not use carnal weapons, but only the "weapons" of prayer and the word of God. (Martin

Luther, for example, when invited to join up with an armed resistance in Germany called the Peasants Revolt, refused to take up carnal weapons. He insisted that he was permitted to use only the weapons of Christ: prayer and the word of God.)

Too Many Masters

When we have Jesus as Lord, He becomes our one and only Master. Jesus does not give anyone else the right to lord it over us. Nor does He give us the right to lord it over anyone else. This awareness greatly simplifies human relationships, and removes most of the stress in life.

On the one hand, we learn to give up our self-made systems of domination and control. These systems create much evil. When people become Christians but do not give up these systems, they are only pasting Jesus' name over the slave ships they have built, and that only makes things worse. The judgment against us is doubled, not removed, by pasting the name *Jesus* on the outside of our systems of domination and control. The King objects: "Why do you call me, 'Lord, Lord,' but you don't do what I say?" (See Mt. 7:21-23.)

Those who truly follow Jesus will resist this urge to dominate and control people. Nothing demolishes the witness of His Church more quickly than this poison creeping into our life together. Nothing damages perceptions of Jesus more tragically. Nothing destroys love and unity more quickly. Any teaching that leads in this direction is to be resisted. We must learn how to live in the opposite spirit, the Spirit of Christ. "Serve one another in love" (Gal. 5:13).

On the other side of the surrendered life, we can enjoy real freedom. "It is for freedom that Christ has set us free" (Gal. 5:1). We do not have to worry so much about what other people think, and we have solid ground to stand on, to resist their manipulations. Nothing stresses us out like ten different people all telling us what to do if we are going to please them; be good people; gain success in life; keep from losing their love. Having only one Master sets us free from all of the little masters, and we can have peace.

Only One Mediator

Let's be clear about this. The Bible explicitly says that there is only one mediator between us and God, the man Christ Jesus (1 Tim. 2:5). Yes, we can have other people who are "over us in the Lord," but that is not an invitation for domination and control. It affirms a disciple-making relationship, and the aim of all disciple-making is to make people dependent on Jesus, not on us. Jesus alone is the Way, the Truth and the Life.

This, by the way, was the bitter lesson of the Shepherding movement, also known as the Discipleship movement, which grew out of the charismatic movement of the '70's. Just when charismatic leaders were helping people discern the moving of the Holy Spirit, a teaching was introduced to the effect that all Christians should have a "shepherd" who is "over them in the Lord." That person would then be the channel through which all of God's words and blessings would flow. This teaching introduced an almost militaristic chain of command into Christian relationships.

The leaders who introduced these doctrines were sincere men and women who had been mightily used of God in millions of lives, including my own. They were trying to counteract a spirit of rebellion and anarchy that they felt was taking over the country during the '60's. Their teaching was based on an interpretation of Scripture and was a sincere attempt to help people follow Jesus.

Yet through these teachings, a spirit of domination and control entered in and did real damage to a great many new believers, who were taught not to depend on Christ in the power of the Holy Spirit, but upon their "shepherd." This was an open invitation to spiritual abuse. Those who taught this hard-wired "chain of command" system later had to apologize for the enormous damage that was done. What began in the Spirit ended in the flesh.

Turf Wars

Another reason why surrender to Jesus makes sense is this: without it, we become rival gangs, all trying to gain control of turf. This is not a pretty scene. Richmond has a long history of gangs. In the days following the Civil War, this is how the spirit of domination and control manifested its presence:

> *...The Richmond gangs known as "cats" were having rock battles in all parts of town. Such sinister aggregations as the Gamble Hill Cats, Oregon Hill Cats, Sidney Cats, Brook Road Cats, Basin Bank Cats, First Street Cats, Second Street Cats, Fourth Street Horribles, Fifth Street Cats, Shockoe Hill Cats, Butchertown Cats, Old Market Cats, Church Hill Cats, Clyde Row Gang, Hobo Gang and Park Sparrows, who roosted in the vicinity of Monroe Park, were among those engaged in this internecine warfare.*[2]

Because the Church of Jesus Christ did not know how to bring healing of the land in Richmond, the false spirit retained the right to divide the city into plots of turf, and say to the young people of the city, "Let's you and him fight."

Often, the Christian Church, rather than challenging these patterns and replacing them with the pattern of Christ, has engaged in its own turf battles. Racial groups and denominations stake their claims over pieces of the city and the various socio-economic classes that inhabit them. Each tries to retain control of that turf against the other gangs. Pastors stake their claims over people, believing that they, the shepherds, have exclusive rights over the people and their money.

What authority do we have with God to ask Him to deal with Richmond's gangs if we ourselves are infected with the same spirit? God is inviting us to surrender our ambitions, rivalries, our need for security and provision to Him and trust Him.

Useful to God

Finally, surrendered people are the only people who can be useful to God during a spiritual awakening. God wants leaders He can trust to disciple new Christians. He cannot trust those new Christians into the care of people who have unsurrendered lives, because they would "beat the sheep." If the promises I am about to articulate have any merit, God is urgently looking for leaders who have surrendered their lives to him, who live by the opposite spirit from the spirit of domination and control.

■ ■ ■

Chapter Twelve

RICHMOND: GATEWAY, REFUGE AND BRIDGE

In the late '70's, God began calling to several Christian leaders to pray for another great awakening. He called to Bill Bright, founder of Campus Crusade for Christ ministries, who began stirring Christians to pray and fast for Revival in America. Campus Crusade produced an important video featuring a lifetime of research by Professor J. Edwin Orr into the cause-and-effect relationship between intensive prayer and spiritual awakening.

God called to David Bryant, who established the Concerts of Prayer movement, drawing Christians together across denominational and racial lines to agree in prayer over cities. David Bryant has held concerts of prayer in many American cities including Richmond.

God called to Pastor Mike Bickle in Kansas City, Missouri, to begin night-and-day prayer leading to a spiritual awakening in our country. Mike's work in prayer and worship has resulted in the International House of Prayer in Kansas City, which has been doing prayer and worship 24/7 for six years at the time of this writing.

Praying for an Awakening

In 1982, my wife and I, tucked away in a little corner of Oregon, received a similar call—to spend two hours in prayer each morning at 5 a.m., to pray for a great awakening in America. This call was confirmed two days after we received it when the oven timer in our kitchen sounded an alarm at 4:59 a.m. This mysterious alarm seemed like a modern day version of a trumpet call. Our faithfulness to this calling is the only reason I can think of why we should have been entrusted with the vision for Richmond that I am about to impart in these pages.

In May of 2004, we were attending a talk in Richmond by Rhonda Hughey from the International House of Prayer in Kansas City. After her talk, a stranger approached us, saying that she had a word from the Lord for us. She read a passage from Luke 2 describing Simeon, a man of prayer who, at the end of his life, saw the answers to his prayer—the newborn Messiah. The word this woman gave us was: "You are a true Simeon, and you will see with your own eyes the answer to your prayers."

The next day, Rhonda invited us to spend a few months at the International House of Prayer. We sensed that God was in this invitation, so we signed up for two months in the "Simeon Company," their internship for people over 55.

Soon after we arrived, the 20 or so interns of the Simeon Company were given a talk on the nature of prophecy. Then several of the intercessors gifted in prophecy began to prophesy over the group. A woman named Sandy Hall looked at me and said, "You, sir, are a true Simeon, and you will see with your own eyes the answer to your prayers." In this way, God confirmed that the great burden of our prayers—a Third Great Awakening—is about to receive an answer that we will see with our eyes. I believe this answer is imminent.

God Wants To Awaken Us

Many others have received words about a great spiritual awakening that is imminent. The following story is from Mike Bickle:

> *On May 28, 1983, the last day of the twenty-one days of prayer and fasting, Bob Jones stood up in a group of about five hundred people and gave a dramatic prophetic word. He said that there would be a drought over Kansas City for three months during that summer. Indeed, a drought did occur from the end of June to the end of September that year. He went on to say that it would rain, however, precisely on August 23. He said this was to be a prophetic sign to us that we should not grow weary in waiting for the precise timing of the spiritual drought over the nation to end.*

Just as the natural drought over Kansas City was to be divinely interrupted on a predetermined day, the spiritual drought would also be divinely interrupted precisely at the appointed time. Consequently, our fasting and prayer, along with the intercession of many others across the nation, was not in vain. God wanted us to understand that there was a precise divine timing of the coming release of the Holy Spirit on the church in America and that this revival was strategically in His hands.

…Though the drought in Kansas City did not begin immediately (there was rain in the month of June), by the end of June the heavens closed. For the month of July and for the first three weeks of August there was almost no rain. By that time I had become an expert weather watcher, and I knew that on August 23rd there was no prediction for rain.

…Our church was scheduled to gather for a meeting the evening of August 23rd. Just before the church meeting began, there came a tremendous downpour of rain for almost an hour. Everyone was shouting and praising God. The drought continued the next day and lasted another five weeks—three months in all, as prophesied, with the exception of August 23rd. It was the third driest summer on record for Kansas City in approximately one hundred years.

...The confirmation of the prophetic word by acts of God in nature has strengthened our faith to believe that just as the rain came precisely on the day predicted, the spiritual rain will come precisely at the divinely appointed time.[1]

God Is Going To Reverse History

Last spring, I was reading Henry M. Ward's book, *Richmond: An Illustrated History*. As I have described in the pages above, Professor Ward described Richmond first as a *gateway*, then as a *city of refuge*. As I read these words, I sensed the Lord saying, "I am going to make Richmond my kind of gateway, and my kind of city of refuge."

God wants to demonstrate at the end of the age His surpassing power for us who believe. Because Richmond has been a gateway that the false spirit has often used in bringing domination and control, God wants to make Richmond a gateway city for the coming mercies of God's love. Just as Richmond was a last-ditch refuge for people desperate to remain in control, God wants to make Richmond a city of refuge for people who are desperate to find grace and mercy by the power of God.

Another word has continued to grow as a certainty, a word spoken over this city almost 20 years ago—that there would be *a spiritual bridge* between Richmond and the nations of West Africa. This prophecy, spoken by Rowland Evans of World Horizons, intimated that people deeply converted to Christ in this city will flow in large numbers to bring God's kindnesses to West Africans. This will be God's answer to the slave traffic that crossed the same ocean two hundred years ago in the opposite direction.

The slave trade in this country cannot remain unanswered. There must be freedom ships that go back to Africa to show the true way of freedom: "It is for freedom that Christ has set us free. Stand firm, then, and do not let yourselves be burdened again by a yoke of slavery" (Gal. 5:1).

Gateway, City of Refuge and Bridge. God wants to turn the last bastion of bondage during the Civil War into a refuge of Christian love and liberty, even when surrounding areas may be losing track of their liberty. This will happen not by human scheming, reasoning, planning or power—but by the power of God. We must ask ourselves: if these three words constitute a true vision for the future of Richmond, how are we to co-operate with what God wants to do?

FOUR BASICS

I believe that four basic beliefs must return into our belief systems as this takes place. These may not be common beliefs today, but they are foundations in the word of God. When all our faddish ideas have passed out of circulation, the word of God will remain forever.

Jesus Is Lord

1 *First*, we must understand that Jesus Christ has risen to a place of ultimate, supreme authority over the world, over world history, over international squabbles and over the tiniest affairs of the most banal of lives. "All authority in heaven and on earth has been given to me," Jesus said (Mt. 28:18).

The apostle Paul, who received the basic teaching of Christ directly from the Lord after His conversion, affirmed this position of Jesus:

> *He is the image of the invisible God, the firstborn over all creation. For by him all things were created: things in heaven and on earth, visible and invisible, whether thrones or powers or rulers or authorities; all things were created by him and for him. He is before all things, and in him all things hold together. (Col. 1:13-17)*

The apostle John saw this Jesus while he was suffering for Him on the Isle of Patmos during the reign of Domitian:

> *I turned around to see the voice that was speaking to me. And when I turned I saw seven golden lampstands, and among the lampstands was someone "like a son of man," dressed in a robe reaching down to his feet and with a golden sash around his chest. His head and hair were white like wool, as white as snow, and his eyes*

were like blazing fire. His feet were like bronze glowing in a furnace, and his voice was like the sound of rushing waters. In his right hand he held seven stars, and out of his mouth came a sharp double-edged sword. His face was like the sun shining in all its brilliance.

When I saw him, I fell at his feet as though dead. (Rev. 1:12-17a)

The first basic belief, then, is that Jesus has risen from a place of lowliness to a position of ultimate and unequalled power and authority, not only over our personal lives, but of world affairs.

Importance of the Church to a City

2 The *second* basic belief is that He wields His authority for the Church wherever it may exist. He is constantly drawing believers together and putting them into relationship with each other called "ligaments" and "tendons." Together we form the Body of Christ, the Bride of Christ. Jesus is the Head of the Church, the Bridegroom of the Bride. The Church, with all its faults and foibles, weaknesses and waywardness, is still the chosen people of God in this present era. God knows the ones who belong to Him and love Him. They have various denominational labels—or some have none at all—and they come from every imaginable racial and cultural group throughout the world.

In every American city, Jesus has His Church. Because the Church is related to Jesus in a unique way, the Church must recognize, grow into, and become worthy of their authority and calling. Jesus wants to use Christian people as a vehicle of blessing for the cities in which they live. The main calling on these people is prayer leading to other ministries as He directs by His wisdom, power and authority.

I pray also that the eyes of your heart may be enlightened in order that you may know the hope to which he has called you, the riches of his glorious inheritance in the saints, and his incomparably great power for us who believe. That power is like the working of his mighty strength, which he exerted in Christ when he raised him from the dead and seated him at his right hand in the heavenly realms, far above all rule and authority, power and dominion, and every title that can be given, not only in the present age but also in the one to come. And God placed all things under his feet and appointed him to be head over everything for the church, which is his body, the fullness of him who fills everything in every way. (Eph. 1:17-23)

Martin Luther put it this way:

In both the spiritual and the temporal realms the very greatest works in the world—even though they are not recognized and acknowledged as such—are continuously performed by Christians. Among these works are the destruction of the

devil's realm, the deliverance of souls, the
conversion of hearts, victory, the preservation of
peace in the land and nation, help, protection,
and salvation in all sorts of distress and
emergencies. All this, Christ says, is to come to
pass through the Christians, because they believe
in Him and derive everything from Him as their
Head. …Therefore it may all be called the
Christians' works and wonders, which they
perform until the last Day.[2]

The Church Is to Seek God's Kingdom

3 The Church's true calling is not to become rich and successful, but to seek God's Kingdom in the city in which it is placed.

The Kingdom of God is a person: Jesus. When people in a city are connected to Jesus the King, and doing what He says, the Kingdom of God has come to that city. The Church, in a time of awakening, must be prepared to take in a harvest—that is, to receive large numbers of people and help them to be connected to the King, listening to Him every day of their lives. It must structure itself for effectiveness in this harvest—equipping people in how to model out, train and teach people to follow the loving ways of Christ. Needless to say, this involves a good deal more than attending an hour's worship service one day a week.

Maturity Means Being Like Jesus

4 An immature Church, unskilled in surrendering to the Lordship of Christ, is incapable of making disciples in a time of awakening. Maturity in Christ is the most important factor in being able to fulfill the Great Commission of the Church: "Go make disciples." An oak tree that is just two years old does not yet produce acorns. It normally takes several years of learning to follow Jesus before a person becomes mature enough to disciple others. Learning to listen to Jesus and have His word abiding in our hearts is a simple requirement—but it is a requirement. We do not need to attend seminary, or be perfect, or pray two hours a day, or be unusually extroverted in order to effectively do the Great Commission. But we do need to be a little experienced in surrendering our lives to Jesus, if we are going to show others how to do this.

■ ■ ■

Chapter Thirteen

THE WISDOM OF EZRA

Let me now share a little more of the story of how I gained a fresh vision for Richmond. I do this as one who submits a vision to others for testing. I hope that others will sense something similar from God, and that what I write will strike a chord of familiarity, if it is right.

High-priestly Incense

As my wife and I devoted ourselves to prayer and fasting at the International House of Prayer in Kansas City, we found ourselves in an extremely productive time, during which the Lord re-shaped our lives, gave us a new vision for the rest of our lives, and showed us a bit of His desire for Richmond.

How well I remember the day, during the first Saturday of August, 2004, when God fulfilled a promise he had made to me the first week of March: "you will get a new mantle." I was seated in the seminar room at the House of Prayer with a group of people who had just finished an all-morning seminar. We were sitting still, listening for a word from the Lord. Suddenly, I began to smell incense very strongly. I looked around. There was no physical reason for this aroma—no one uncorking their anointing oil. My wife also smelled the incense, but no one else smelled it, only the two of us. Then two words came from other people in the room to me:

"I saw Jesus come up to you and hug you."

"I saw you getting a priest's robe. Then I saw you swinging a censer back and forth, with incense coming out of it."

Clearly, God had spoken an "aroma-word" to my nose, confirmed and interpreted by two conventionally spoken words from two other people. So I began to ask, "Lord, what is a priest's robe? What are you doing in my life? You seem to be giving me the mantle of a priest. But what is a priest?"

He replied with His "still small voice," strong and urgent: "Read First and Second Chronicles."

The following Monday was the first day of a monthly "global bridegroom fast" in the community. Carla and I decided to seclude ourselves in our quarters at the

Hernnhut apartments, to pray and fast and read Chronicles. As I did, the Holy Spirit interpreted these ancient books to my heart. I began to realize that I was indeed gaining a new mantle, a priest's robe, a priestly calling. God was using Ezra to instruct me.

A Hidden Treasure Discovered

As I secluded myself with God, I received from Ezra foundational principles for cities, that have been locked away in our scriptures for centuries. As I sat before the Lord, the two historical books Ezra wrote were transformed before my eyes from the least interesting books of the Bible (full of genealogies and repetitive history), to the most interesting and relevant for city-wide leadership.

In particular, Ezra focuses our gaze on two underlying principles, which are relevant for cities like Richmond:

1. The importance of preserving the unity of God's people, not at the cost of compromising truth, but at the cost of learning deep humility with one another. Humility, not compromise, is the true price of oneness.

2. The necessity of restoring the ministry of the priest, who ministers petition, praise and thanksgiving to the Lord. Here the focus is entirely on ministering *to the Lord* in fulfillment of the First Commandment.

The neglect of these two principles in the practice of Christian living has been catastrophic for us Americans. Ezra was confronted with the same reality in his day, so he spent most of his energy restoring these two principles to everyday life as David had done before him. In fact, King David was the source of most of Ezra's inspiration, just as Ezra can be ours.

Unity Through Humility

The way to achieve unity is not through compromise, but through humility. In the life of David and Ezra, we see the struggle to draw Israel together without compromising the basic truth of what God had revealed to His people.

Ezra started out by acknowledging certain truth on which there could be no compromise. God had given David a unique anointing, and had shown David how to put God first in all things. Under the divided monarchy, the northern kingdom had compromised those principles, forming themselves into a secessionist movement. While resisting all attempts to compromise God's revealed word about the Temple, the sacrifices, the anointing of Davidic leaders, and the God-ordained protocols, Ezra was careful to reach out to northern secessionists when their heart was to observe God's ways. He did this through identificational repentance, confessing the sin of all Israel as though it were his own, saying, "Not one of us can stand in your presence." He did not take a superior or accusatory attitude toward his northern brothers (as the Pharisees and Sadducees of Jesus' day did later).

King David's Example

Five hundred years before Ezra arrived on the scene, David had struggled to reach out to unite Israel without compromising basic principles. David had to find a way to win over the hearts of those who had followed King Saul, but without making the compromises Saul had made. Saul had not learned to seek God, had not been sensitive to the voice of God, but had been guided by a spirit of domination and control, and the fear of losing control. Ironically, the more he gave in to his fears, the more his worst fears were realized. His inability either to listen to the still small voice of God, to consult the means of guidance available to him, or to follow the plain directives of the prophet Samuel, proved catastrophic, even to murdering God's priests at Nob.

Yet David never said, "Saul does not deserve to be king. God has chosen me now. I will seize the kingdom for myself." At no point did David show the least desire to seize the kingdom, even though he had been anointed king early in life. His attitude was, "If God wants me to be king, I will be king. If not, I won't." The still small voice of God told him consistently that he had to humble himself, allowing himself to be chased around all creation by the armies of Saul, learning how to trust God, and respect the office that Saul still held.

An important lesson in humility.

During those years of refining, most of Israel refused to support David. They knew which side their bread was buttered on. They did not support David until it was to their advantage to do so. Yet later, David, in consolidating the nation, reached out to those who had served Saul, humbly forgiving years of persecution and dishonor, inviting them to participate in the prosperity of the Davidic anointing. When he became king, David allowed Abner, the commander of Saul's army, to join forces with him. He also took care of Mephibosheth, Saul's lame grandson. Whatever personal humiliation he had to endure for the sake of national unity he was willing to endure. Yet he was also careful to avoid the careless policies of Saul. Humility? Yes! Compromise? No. He loved God too much to compromise His ways.

Later Kings

Likewise, during the later years of the monarchy, Ezra shows how some of the Davidic kings walked this line more successfully than others did. The Davidic king Jehoshaphat, for example, formed an alliance with Ahab. His willingness to confront the policies of Ahab was weak at best. This alliance amounted to an unequal yoking. So God sent a prophet, Micaiah, to warn him about it (2 Chron. 19:1-3). Jehoshaphat had tried to gain unity, but at the price of compromise.

Amaziah likewise wanted to form a league with Israel in his battle against Edom. God told him that this alliance amounted to compromise, so he forsook it—at risk of angering his potential allies (2 Chron. 25:7-10). He was forced to sacrifice unity for the sake of faithfulness to God. He wanted unity, but it was not worth the price required of him, so he abandoned the idea.

On the other side of the coin, Hezekiah successfully reached out to their northern kinsmen without compromising basic principles. "Hezekiah sent word to all Israel and Judah and also wrote letters to Ephraim and Manasseh, inviting them to come to the temple of the Lord in Jerusalem and celebrate the Passover to the Lord" (2 Chron. 30:1). Here was an attempt to reunite Israel around the commandments and worship of God without compromise. King Josiah, likewise, humbly reached out to the northern tribes for a greater unity without compromising basic principles (2 Chron. 35:18).

Whom Do We Follow?

How do these ideas about unity apply to us today? There have been many occasions when we Americans, including those of us in Richmond, have allowed our Christian faith and heritage to become an opportunity for pride, even bullying. Our treatment of Native Americans in the tragic history of Indian boarding schools is an example.

These tragic mistakes, however, should not become a reason to compromise what we know about Jesus, whom we call the Christ, the Anointed One. By calling Him Christ, we are saying that He is God's choice to be Lord of all. We are saying that He is the only one who deserves our ultimate obedience, the full surrender of our lives, our allegiance.

Either Jesus is Lord of all, or He is not, in which case we should stop calling him Christ. To suggest that all faiths are equally valid pathways to the same God is to confuse humility with compromise. The antidote to pride is not compromise, but humility, and we must take care to discern the difference. We today are faced with the same ticklish issue of David and Ezra, how to demonstrate humility without compromise.

In my review of Richmond history, I have showed that Christian people have often confused the Spirit of Christ with the spirit of domination and control. This tragic lack of discernment created many horrors and the name of Christ became associated with those horrors. The temptation in this situation is to conclude that it is not important for us to follow Jesus. "Look at what Christians did in the past. So it's not important to follow Christ."

The right response, however, is to admit that we have followed Jesus poorly at times, repent of our need to be in control of other peoples' lives and destinies, surrender our lives to God as best we can, and walk in humility. And never compromise the truth about Jesus.

We must repent of spiritual pride, because God does not honor people who are proud toward each other or toward people of other faiths. But allowing compromise about who Jesus is—this would not be a step in the right direction. It would be a mistaken way of retreating from the mistakes of our past. One mistake heaped on another.

According to Ephesians 1:10, only Jesus has the power to unite all things. We must never compromise this basic hope.

■ ■ ■

Chapter Fourteen

SPIRITUAL LEADERSHIP OF A CITY

Much attention has recently been given to restoring the five-fold ministry mentioned in Ephesians 4—apostles, prophets, evangelists, pastors and teachers. This is the five-fold ministry of the Church, and the Church is not complete without it. However, as we turn to the city-wide level, as opposed to the level of Church reformation, we must awaken to the city-wide offices that are evident in Chronicles. If God is wanting to build cities "whose architect and builder is God," then we must pay closer attention to the offices of spiritual leadership in cities.

Prophet, Priest and King

In Ezra's day, leadership was divided into three offices: prophet, priest and king. Some leaders were called to minister God's truth outward among the people. They were prophets. Others were called to minister to the Lord. They were priests. Others were called to oversee the affairs of state—as kings and governors. Each type of leadership required its own unique gifting.

Normally, the three offices were distinct from each other. Though from time to time God called some priests into prophetic leadership, this sort of thing was the exception, not the rule. Most of the time, we see danger when one office tries to absorb another office, to take it over. This was especially true when kings tried to take over and control the other two offices.

When prophet, priest and king were in good relationship to each other—when they humbly listened to each other without trying to control each other—all went well. For example, in 2 Chronicles 24, there was a healthy interaction between King Joash and Jehoiada the high priest. Joash wanted to restore the temple in Jerusalem. When Jehoiada failed to listen to the young king, Joash confronted him. Because Jehoiada humbled himself before the Lord, whom they both served, a relationship of mutual respect grew up between them, and the two accomplished much. The city and the nation were blessed. Jehoiada provided for the young king a safe environment, but did not use his position to control the king.

Unfortunately, when Jehoiada died, the fruitful alliance was broken, and Joash fell away into compromise. God then turned to His prophets to bring correction, but Joash also refused to listen to them. He became hardened in his old age. As a result, the blessing of God was withdrawn.

We see a similar pattern in King Asa, who was faithful in his early years to humble himself with the priests and prophets of his day. But prosperity made him proud and he later lost God's blessing, as is the certain result of an arrogant heart. God never exalts the proud.

Many people believe that Old Testament government was an absolute monarchy or a theocracy. In reality, we see a separation of powers in leadership, similar to what we enjoy in our country today among the legislative, executive and judicial branches. God required mutual submission among a triumvirate of leaders, each charged with an area of responsibility and authority from God.

Separation of Powers

The separation of these powers in a relationship of mutual respect was God's will in Israel. God was very aware of the spirit of domination and control, and the potential for the abuse of absolute power. As I have mentioned, He had specifically warned Samuel about this early in the monarchy (1 Sam. 8).

Pride became a huge problem among leaders. Pride could manifest itself in two ways. First, a leader would try to take over and control the other offices, as when a king brought the prophets into his palace, paid them a salary, and controlled what they would say until it was completely agreeable to himself. Or, second, pride could cause a leader to neglect, disdain and ignore the other offices.

Humility, on the other hand, led to healthy relationships of mutual honoring, in which each leader listened to what God was doing in the other two offices. There would be neither disdain for, nor control of, the other two God-ordained leaders.

Ezra showed how King David had related to the prophets and priests of his day in a lifestyle of humility. David demonstrated this spirit every time he was confronted by the prophets of his day, Samuel, Nathan and Gad. On the one hand, he always listened to them with respect. On the other, he never tried to control them.

Also, David established the priests as valuable allies, in a way Saul had never done. He placed the priests not on Mount Zion, his own mountain, but on Mount Moriah, a place with a separate identity. David purchased materials for the temple, but he did so as a private citizen, and the priests were never beholden to David for their daily living. God provided for them by means of the tithe from all the people.

There is no evidence that David ever invited the priests to his palace to start meetings with prayer. David was a believer in his own right, and was respected as such. He did not need a clergyman to validate his decisions. He himself was a follower of God. On the other hand, He fully recognized the value of the priests' ministry of love, and encouraged it every way he could. Here is a delicate balance of leadership and mutual respect, nurtured by good communication.

The Three Offices of Christ

How do these principles affect us, who belong to Christ, today? Jesus drew the three offices—prophet, priest and king—into Himself. He became the fulfillment of all three.

As a prophet, He was the fulfillment of Mosaic prophecy in Deuteronomy 18:14-15: "The Lord your God will raise up for you a prophet like me from among your own brothers. You must listen to him." (See Acts 3:22. Jesus fulfills this prophecy.) He was the ultimate high priest "after the order of Melchizedek" (Heb. 7). He was also the ultimate king referred to in Daniel 2, a literal Son of David; "and the government is on His shoulders" (Is. 9:7).

After He rose from the dead, He bequeathed these offices to His people, appointing His New Covenant people to wield authority as prophets, priests and kings. The Holy Spirit takes what belongs to Jesus and makes it known to us (Jn. 16:15). The authority of prophet, priest and king is one of Jesus' richest blessings to His people.

Every Christian is all three of these in our little areas of personal life. We can learn to stand in the authority of who we are, if only we know who we are *in Christ*—prophets, priests and kings. We receive revealed truth from God to speak into a deceived world, which makes us prophets. "I want you all to speak in tongues, but even more to prophesy," wrote Paul (1 Cor.14:5).

Every Christian is also a priest, equipped by the Holy Spirit to be a "royal priesthood" ministering thanks, praise and petition in God's very presence (1 Pet. 2:5). We are to learn how to relate to God at an intimate level, to be constantly in prayer, to have a God-song in our hearts always, and to allow Him to down-load to us His burdens, griefs, joys and love.

We are also to learn how to reign on earth as kings, or as "kings' kids" as we used to say years ago (Rev. 5:10). He has built a world that operates by moral laws, as well as by natural laws. If we ignore those moral laws, violating our conscience, we will only bring curses down on ourselves, and invite demonic infestation in our hearts, our households and our cities. On the other hand, if we learn how to rule our bodies, manage our households and govern our cities by the virtues of righteousness, blessings will flow. Look at the video *Let the Seas Resound* to see how this principle operates in a nation. The video *Transformations* shows this principle in operation in cities. These are available from the Sentinel Group, listed in my Afterword.

God Appoints Leaders Over Cities

Though all of us have been given spiritual authority in all three areas, and we are learning how to use that authority in appropriate ways in our personal lives, when it comes to public leadership, the situation changes. Some people are "created in Christ Jesus" for public leadership ministries, but none of us has the spiritual gifts and skills to do all things well in areas of public leadership.

Leaders must discern where in His scheme we fit, and stay in that place. Some fit best as prophets speaking truth to people. Others are gifted to minister as priests to God. Others are best in leadership of government in the city, and in ordering our life together. Though several of the prophets of the Old Testament were drawn from the priestly class, it is rare that people are called to more than one area of public leadership. On the other hand, we have often seen people, out of personal ambition, try to do more than they are really called to do.

Terminology

Let me say a word about terminology. We don't usually use words like "prophet," "priest" and "king" today in public. These words are not common among us on television or in the newspapers. But I will use these words in the broadest New Testament sense and try to recover that sense for today.

If a prophet is one who speaks God's revealed truth into the deception of worldly falsehood, then every time a preacher preaches God's revealed truth, He is fulfilling the office of the prophet. In addition, some people may be raised up today to be seers, with a genuine, specialized gift of seeing into the spirit realm. But I am using the word "prophet" more generally, to refer to all whose calling is to speak God's revealed truth into our culture.

The word "priest" will mean different things in different denominations. But, again, I am using the word as broadly as possible to refer to a ministry like that which

God gave the Levite, which was, at heart, a ministry of praise, thanksgiving and petition (1 Chron. 16:4). This ministry was exclusively a ministry to the Lord. The Levite had God as his portion. He faced toward God, specializing in how to relate to God as a different class of being from himself. You might say it was his responsibility to span the enormous cultural gap between us and God, moving across the bridge that God had built in the temple sacrifices. (Today, God's bridge is Jesus.) The priest's ministry was not to interpret God's word to the people. That was the ministry of the prophet. As a priest, he ministered to God.

The word "king" is, of course, badly out of date among us except in fairy tales and history classes. Belief in the divine right of kings led to terrible abuses of power around the world and we inherited a great many hard lessons about this from our European ancestors. Yet we continue to have government, and God still appoints ruling authorities. Zerubbabel, for example, was not a king in the classical sense, but a governor. As a son of David, he was a type for some today who are mayors, city councilmen and governors. God has still established governing authorities, and they rule by His decree whether they realize it or not (1 Tim. 2:1-2). Therefore, we still need people who know how to wield governing authority under the authority of Christ, who is Lord of all.

Mutual Submission and Cooperation

Having said all this, let's now move on to the main

point. We need in Richmond, still today, three offices, each of which respects the others and sees the need for the others. This message has become confused in Virginia because of our unique history.

Today, the biblical doctrine of mutual separation and humility has morphed, through the mind of Thomas Jefferson, into the so-called "separation of church and state." Jefferson was not building this concept on biblical ideas, but was reacting to domination and control manifested in the Anglican Church. His reaction was justified because the Anglican Church reflected a confusion of kingly and prophetic authority. But his opposition was not based on a clear biblical vision of people working in a healthy relationship to each other. In fact, his ideas have pitted State against Church as though they were bitter enemies of each other.

We must move beyond the fear of domination and control, or of losing control. We must gain a healthy vision of how these three offices are supposed to relate to each other in listening love and mutual honoring. Then we will be in position to become a city of refuge.

■ ■ ■

Chapter Fifteen

AN END-TIME PRIESTHOOD

The separation of, and respect for, all three offices is just as important when we turn to the priestly calling, even though it is the prophet and king that get all the attention in this debate about church and state.

Priestly Ministry and the First Commandment

In our country, the priestly office has been so completely ignored that it has almost ceased to exist. At the heart of this office is the basic calling of ministry *to the Lord*. The priest, in the days of Ezra and David, was called to minister before the Lord night and day so that the fire of love would never go out in the temple of God. The priest made sure that the love of God, the first commandment, was ministered through thanks, praise and petition. (Petition that grows out of worship is best defined as asking God for the desires of God's heart, not ours. Petition, like praise and thanksgiving, becomes a ministry of love, and not merely begging God for what we want.) This ministry was given to the descendants of Levi under the Old Covenant.

God was looking for love, not because He has an enormous ego that requires us to worship Him, but because love always looks for reciprocation. One-way love, by nature, is incomplete. God desires and yearns for our love, just as we are incomplete when we are estranged from Him. Think how incomplete you feel when you love someone who doesn't love you back.

His elevation of the tribe of Levi to this first-commandment ministry was (in God's mind) a great honor. He anticipated that the tribe of Levi would see it as such, and He withheld from them a portion of land as an inheritance, saying, "I am your portion."

I have already traced what happened to this special honor by the time Jesus appeared on the scene—how the chief priests had formed a political party, turned the temple system into a monopoly and greedily grabbed huge tracts of land around Jerusalem. It was to preserve and protect this worldly inheritance that they made covenants with the spirit of domination and control, while their hearts moved farther and farther away from God and His desire for true love.

Men after God's Own Heart

By contrast, a thousand years before, King David, after turning Jerusalem into his capital city, was careful to put the Levites in place as one of his first priorities.

> *He appointed some of the Levites to minister before the ark of the Lord, to make petition, to give thanks, and to praise the Lord, the God of Israel. (1 Chron. 16:4)*

The Levites were appointed to many other duties of temple service, of course, but at heart, all were to support the ministry of asking, thanking and praising. These are the three elements of priestly ministry that carry over into the New Testament.

They did these things for one reason only: God had asked them to do it because it would please His heart. Because David loved the Lord and had become a man after God's own heart, he made sure that the Levites were in the center of his capital, doing what God had asked them to do. He also provided them with his own songs, with instruments he had made and with materials he purchased for his son, Solomon, to use in building a temple.

Ezra, following that example six centuries later, was also careful to establish this ministry of love to the Lord as first priority among the exiles from Babylon. Before there was any attempt to build the walls of Jerusalem, they rebuilt the temple and put the Levites in place. God raised up the prophet Haggai to challenge the people with this top priority.

Is it a time for you yourselves to be living in your paneled houses, while this house remains a ruin? (Hag. 1:4)

Then God put Joshua and Zerubbabel in place, as described by Ezra.

"But What Good Will It Do?"

This ordering of priorities does not make sense by modern American standards. Surely, we would say, it would have been better if they had built their walls first, so they would be safe from enemies. Then the construction of the temple and the priestly ministry could have been carried out in safety in their own proper time.

This is our way of reasoning, but it is not God's. Though the Levitical calling had nothing to do with what we today call "ministry" (taking care of human need), the priesthood in another way was essential for taking care of *all* human need. When God is being loved, He bestows His presence and favor to a community. His presence brings with it all sorts of blessings and protections for people, as David had discovered during his lifetime (I Chron. 29:16).

Without the blessing and manifest presence of God, people do not fare well and cities do not fare well. But with that presence flowing like a river through our living rooms and through the streets of a city, everything fares very well. The *Transformations* videos of George Otis convey the reality of this truth. The power of God is as relevant today as in Bible times.

The most significant lesson I gained from my study of Chronicles is this: Put the first commandment first, and all else flows in proper order. Let the first commandment be ignored, and nothing flows in proper order. This principle applies all the more as we move toward the end of the present age.

Love and Knowledge at the End of the Age

The Bible describes two disturbing trends during this end-time period. First, that most people's love will grow cold (Mt. 24:12); second, that Knowledge will increase (Dan. 12:4). When Daniel prophesied the increase of knowledge at the end of the age, he did not link that with a gradual evolutionary increase of human progress until, at last, the kingdom of God arrives.

The Church of Jesus Christ must stand against this perverse trend, in which knowledge increases but love disappears. The Church must be the last-days community of love, not knowledge. Knowledge puffs up, but love builds up (1 Cor. 8:1).

The power and presence of God come to a city where Christians, desperate for God, cry out to Him day and night as He requested us to do:

> *I have posted watchmen on your walls,*
> *   O Jerusalem;*
> *They will never be silent day or night.*
> *   You who call on the Lord,*
> *Give yourselves no rest,*

*And give him no rest till he establishes Jerusalem
(or Richmond)
And makes her the praise of the earth. (Is. 62:6)*

*...If my people, who are called by my name, will
humble themselves and pray and seek my face
and turn from their wicked ways, then will I hear
from heaven and will forgive their sin and will
heal their land. (2 Chron. 7:14)*

*And foreigners who bind themselves to the Lord
To serve him,
To love the name of the Lord,
And to worship him,
All who keep the Sabbath without desecrating it
And who hold fast to my covenant—
These I will bring to my holy mountain
And give them joy in my house of
prayer. (Is. 56:6-7a)*

Ezra clearly believed that obedience to the first commandment was the key to everything else, even the protection of Jerusalem. That is why he prayed: "He has granted us new life to rebuild the house of our God and repair its ruins, and he has given us a wall of protection in Judah and Jerusalem" (Ez. 9:9). The wall of protection he refers to was God Himself, not bricks and mortar. Nehemiah had not yet arrived on the scene to build the walls of the city.

When love for God wells up from the heart of a city night and day; when saints with hearts aflame with passion for God seek His face together with humility; when believers put away their differences and offenses to become a house of prayer in a city; when Christians stop going off "one to his fields, another to his business," and return love to God as He deserves; then God responds differently to such a city than when all, like sheep, go each to his own way.

Where Are the Priests?

How do we Americans respond, for example, to a passage like Ezekiel 44, where God revealed to the Levites who had fallen into idol worship the consequences of their sin:

> *They are not to come near to serve me as priests or come near any of my holy things or my most holy offerings; they must bear the shame of their detestable practices. Yet I will put them in charge of the duties of the temple and all the work that is to be done in it.*

> *But the priests, who are Levites and descendants of Zadok and who faithfully carried out the duties of my sanctuary when the Israelites went astray from me, are to come near to minister before me…. (Ez. 44:13-15a)*

Most Western pastors are not trained to appreciate priestly ministry. The ministry of the Church has been defined almost entirely as a prophetic or governmental one—that is, a preaching ministry, or ordering our life together. Horizontal, not vertical. Most Western Christians, whether influenced by Martin Luther, or Martin Luther King, when they come to church, are looking for a sermon with practical "things to do." Most pastors have come into pastoral ministry today to meet that need because they feel the inner urging of the prophet or they wish to change the world and do some practical good for people.

When you put pastors together in a room, they will inevitably start preaching to each other some fresh insight God has given them. Put them into a prayer meeting and they will turn it into a preaching service. They will invite speakers to it, so that everyone will have a proper understanding of what God's word says about prayer. They will teach and preach on prayer but they will not pray.

In these circles, when Christians with a true priestly calling are present, they will at first feel frustrated, then angry, then perhaps even a little rebellious, because their shepherds, their leaders, are interfering with the priestly calling, and are making no provision for it. In fact, they are taking the very setting designed for praise, prayer and thanksgiving, and filling it with talk, so much talk that the "Levite" cannot get a word of real prayer, praise or thanksgiving in edgewise.

Separation of Priest and Prophet

Here we see the need to keep proper order between the priest and the prophet. Once again, we must have a separation, so that each office can function as it was designed. Praise and prayer have their own validity. They are not just a warm-up for the main course—preaching. God deserves to be loved in His own right, and He is appointing a class of people today who are becoming sensitive to this truth. These He is raising up to be an end-time priesthood. They are given a genuine call to put the first commandment first.

Let each office have a humble respect for the other. Let them provide for each other and listen to each other so the Church may be complete in its ministry to the city.

Learning the Value of Cooperation

Prophets, priests and kings tend to want to act independently of one another. It is only natural for each type of leader to think that his own type of leadership is the one that causes the sun to rise and fall on our city.

Preachers believe that effectiveness in proclaiming God's word surely depends on the quality of their public speaking. However, history indicates that effectiveness may depend more on whether they have intercessors praying at the same time they are preaching.

C.H. Spurgeon, who ministered following the awakening of 1857-8, positioned teams of intercessors in the basement of the assembly halls where he preached. He was known as the most effective preacher of his day.

When I read Finney's sermons today, they seem so dry, lawyerly and matter-of-fact. Yet Finney's results were astonishing, as recorded in his *Memoirs*. How could these sermons have won so many hearts, I ask myself.

The answer? Finney would send Father Nash, his chief intercessor, ahead of himself, to stir up prayer in cities where he was scheduled to preach.

Things go better when we learn to cooperate in the work of God's kingdom. God's kingdom does not depend on any one person, no matter how gifted or how thoroughly educated.

■ ■ ■

Chapter Sixteen

A HOUSE OF PRAYER IN RICHMOND

I have said that the priestly calling is one that restores the first commandment to its rightful place, as top priority. Now let's follow that point to its logical conclusion. It is love that draws down the power and presence of God into a city. God is like us—or rather, we are built like God. We go wherever we believe we are loved. God, too, is attracted to love relationships, and He is grieved and repelled where domination and control hurt people. If we want God to bestow blessing on our city, we must pay attention to whether we are loving God with all our heart, mind, soul and strength.

The Business-like Church

The love of God must precede all human loves, or our human loves will spin out of control and become idolatrous. Human loves, even marital love, will go off track if not placed in the parentheses of the love of God. When the love of God is neglected in a culture, that culture turns to false comforts and becomes consumed with obsessions, addictions, escapist entertainment, isolation, performance orientation—the human heart trying desperately to fill the void with things our minds have invented for the purpose. The society that rejects and ignores the priestly calling is a society in deep trouble. Ours is such a society.

Unfortunately, the Church has not resisted the tendency to move toward idolatrous loves. The pure expression of love toward God–the ministry of the priesthood–has been marginalized in American churches. Most people come to our churches because they believe that they will "get something out of it." If they do not feel that they have been rewarded, they will go elsewhere on Sunday morning. The idea that they have been called by Jesus into a royal priesthood to minister love to God would be completely foreign to their way of thinking. In fact, they do not even have categories with which to talk about such things.

Everything in American life has become utilitarian— "what can I get out of this?" Even worship takes on the atmosphere of entertainment, as though the purpose is to make *us* feel good. We have forgotten not only how to love God. We have forgotten how to love. Our culture has turned into a business, and the Church has followed the trend.

A Slow Awakening to Praise

But God is not abandoning us to this businesslike mentality. He is asking us to love again. Some who have heard His voice have been particularly called to minister love back to Him in a true priestly ministry. Those who have experienced this know who they are. No one has to explain it to them. To them, it is simply a deep truth that has emerged into their lives without rational explanation. Worship, prayer and thanksgiving are shut up in their bones, trying to find expression.

During the last thirty years, since the days of Merlin Carothers and his books about the life of praise, the priestly calling has been slowly making a comeback among Christians. Worship services, once narrowly confined to three doctrinal hymns, a sermon and an offering with announcements, have been extended to two hours to make room for the many love songs composed by Christian songwriters today. Now it is time to take the next step in Richmond: to establish a priesthood ministering to the Lord 24/7 in a house of prayer.

City-wide Houses of Prayer

Last summer, I spent two months in such a community in Kansas City. God is raising up houses of prayer like this all over the world, in city after city. Hardly a month goes by that I don't hear of another example. Recently, my friend, Andrew Fuller went on a World Horizons trip to Beirut, Lebanon, and reported that there is a fledgling 24/7 prayer center growing up there. Tom White has been touring the world building prayer in such far-flung places as Katmandu, St. Petersburg, Jerusalem, New Delhi and Tokyo. Tom's book, *City-wide Prayer Movements,* takes a look at what God is doing around the world, raising up, in various formats, city-wide prayer movements. This comes from the simultaneous calling of God to scattered and diverse people groups all over the world, and it is not organized by human design.

Here in Richmond, Common Thread ministries, led by Matthew and Sherrie Moore, have spearheaded this movement. In Richmond, it is taking a unique form, different from that in Kansas City, where a single leader, Mike Bickle, has produced the prayer center. Here in Richmond, the aim is to produce a ministry that is not owned and controlled by any one denomination or Christian culture, but will be an expression of prayer and worship by the whole Church at Richmond, "whosoever will." Can we dare to believe that such a thing is possible?—a fiery furnace of devotion expressing *on behalf of the whole Body of Christ in Richmond* the love Jesus deserves? Visit the website of the Richmond International House of Prayer to gain the latest developments as this vision becomes reality in Richmond (RIHOP.com)

Love and Prayer, the Dynamic Duo

Of course, we can all say that we don't need such a ministry here. All we need to do is to have more worship in our separate congregations and denominations.

In theory, that is true. But it is not only prayer that we need in Richmond, it is a demonstration of love. Prayer that is spoken in a spirit of turfism and bitter competition among Christians will only grieve the Holy Spirit more than He has already been grieved in this city. What we need is that unique combination of loving prayer, loving thanksgiving and loving worship that arises from a unified Body of believers. In the end, Jesus is still looking to fulfill the answer to His high priestly prayer:

> *May they be brought to complete unity to let the world know that you sent me, and have loved them even as you have loved me.*

> *...I have made you known to them and will continue to make you known in order that the love you have for me may be in them and that I myself may be in them. (Jn. 17:23b, 26)*

To build a house of prayer the way I have described would be a challenge to our love, yes. But it is just such a challenge that God is laying before us today. Jesus predicted that massive miracles and raisings from the dead would not be enough to convince a skeptical world about Him (Lk. 16:31). But a unified Church would (Jn. 17:21). A unified Church is the greatest miracle of all, a miracle of the heart, which Jesus wants to present to the world at the end of the age. This can only rise out of a common experience of the unconditional love of Jesus. Christianity is not a religion, it is a relationship based on His love, which is higher, deeper, longer-lasting and wider than ours.

The present separations by race and denomination reflect our will, not God's. They also reflect our historic participation in past moves of God. Most of our denominations were born during one or another of the great awakenings of the past.

Unfortunately, each move of God, though proven to be divinely ordained by its results, was invariably opposed by other older denominations when it happened—even though those denominations, born in similar moves of God, were opposed by older denominations of an earlier age. In the end, God's wisdom is justified by all her children. Though new moves of God are opposed by old-line groups of Christians for various reasons, the huge numbers of people who have come to Christ through them validate them as genuine. You would think that we would have learned by now not to oppose God, if only out of respect for Jesus' clear warning about blaspheming the Holy Spirit.

At the end of the age, Jesus is looking for the fulfillment of his high priestly prayer. It is time for us Christians to wipe the scales from our eyes, admit that God has been asking us to walk in love, and repent of our pride, separateness and lovelessness. That is the groundwork needed for a new royal priesthood in Richmond.

Identifying the Called Priests Among Us

The role of the priest is the ministry of love toward God. One does not need to be ordained by a denomination to be such a priest. It is the ministry of Anna, of Simeon, of Mary of Bethany who poured sweet oil on the feet of Jesus. We must find the Annas, Simeons and Marys in Richmond, and bring them together to fulfill the calling God has put in their hearts.

> *May the God who gives endurance and encouragement give you a spirit of unity among yourselves as you follow Christ Jesus, so that with one heart and mouth you may glorify the God and Father of our Lord Jesus Christ. (Rom. 15:5-6)*

Pastors who see the necessity for a royal priesthood ministering to the Lord in the heart of Richmond will identify those in their congregations who have a priestly heart, and will release them into a city-wide ministry of praise, prayer and thanksgiving night and day.

In this effort, we must convert congregational and cultural distinctives from a curse that separates, to a blessing of mutual honoring. Black, white, Asian, Native and Hispanic cultures (just to mention the main ones in Richmond) each have their distinctives precious to the Lord. As we allow the Father's love for Jesus to melt our hearts, that love will unite us as siblings, yet our distinctives will remain. We will continue to "be who we are." There must be no attempt by one group to make over the other groups into its own image. The love of the Father for Jesus has the power to unite people of diverse cultures, so that they can praise Him happily as their hearts find expression through their culture.

Attracting the Glory of God

It is this reciprocal love-of-the-Father-for-Jesus flowing through the Body of Christ that attracts the presence of God into a city and eventually heals the land on which the city is built.

When Solomon completed the temple in Jerusalem, and the priests were placed in their stations, God responded by revealing His glory amongst them, at the center of Jerusalem:

> *Then the temple of the Lord was filled with a cloud, and the priests could not perform their service because of the cloud, for the glory of the Lord filled the temple of God. (2 Chron. 513b-14)*

We of Richmond must equip ourselves with an understanding of the mercies that flow from the manifest presence of God's glory—the massive and dramatic conversions, miracles of healing, widespread pursuit of righteousness, healing of ecological curses, emergence of justice, the care of the poor, and the eradication of violence in the streets and homes of our city. The presence of God is something we want in Richmond, even though it will cost us dearly. It will cost us our desire to stay in control.

■ ■ ■

Chapter Seventeen

A CITY NO LONGER CHAINED TO ITS PAST

Richmond is a city with a past. The past shouts from every street in downtown Richmond: beautiful, aristocratic architecture, stately statues of past heroes, shaded parks and a picturesque river with more history than any other river in the country.

Jesus is aware not only of the past, but the future. My sense is that He wants us to gear up for the future, to prepare for yet undreamed of world events. Much of what He is doing in the present—calling to Church and city leaders to co-operate more closely, calling Church denominations and groups to work and pray together—is urgent because of what Jesus knows is just around the next bend of the river. For this reason, we Richmonders must take our eyes off our past, and prepare for the unseen future that Jesus is trying to tell us about.

Jesus and the End-time Church

Speculation about the future is a hobby full of risks and dangers. Yet today Jesus is speaking to many respected leaders about the future, imparting a sense of urgency similar to what I have sensed for Richmond.

In the year 2000, for example, Billy Graham spearheaded a massive gathering in Amsterdam, to which he invited all the heads of the major missions organizations in the world. Attending that meeting were the five-star generals of God's Church, those responsible for completing the Great Commission globally. For the first time, they all came together, heads of missions organizations like Wycliffe Bible Translators, Youth with a Mission, Campus Crusade for Christ, Frontiers, and many denominational missions agencies. As that meeting progressed, it became clear that many leaders were hearing a fresh word from the Lord, who was telling them to vastly shorten their time-tables for completing their work, in fulfillment of Matthew 24:14—"And this gospel of the kingdom will be preached in the whole world as a testimony to all nations, and then the end will come."

For example, Roy Peterson, head of Wycliffe Bible Translators, received instructions from God that Wycliffe should complete their work not in the 125 years they had planned, but in 25. Wycliffe has had to retool their entire organization to fit the new time-table. Other global missions organizations, impassioned by similar fresh directives in the year 2000, are responding similarly today.[1] Everywhere, the global Church seems to be fired up with a sense of urgency.

God wants us to discern the signs of the times, not so we will spend more time writing about signs of the times, but so that we can become a sign of the times. He is preparing a people to fulfill the prophecy of Daniel: "Those who are wise will shine like the brightness of the heavens, and those who lead many to righteousness, like the stars for ever and ever" (Dan. 12:3). Big doings are afoot, and God is calling us out of our safe havens into places of heroism. "The creation waits in eager expectation for the sons of God to be revealed" (Rom. 8:19). God is training us how to be "a kingdom and priests to serve our God," that we may rule on earth (Rev. 5:10). We do not need more books about end-time prophecy. We need a Church ready to re-tool its ministries in obedience to the instructions of the Head.

I believe that many people just now are receiving similar new and unexpected direction from Jesus that is requiring us all to take a fresh look at the future and re-tool our ministries. I believe that the Church at Richmond will soon be required to re-tool even the very concept of what "Church" is. Just as global ministries are required to re-tool to adapt to new instructions, so will we in Richmond.

Cities of Refuge

Though I received in 2004 a sense that God wants to make Richmond a City of Refuge, that does not mean I have a clear idea of what such a city would look like. But let me tell you a bit more of my story.

Two months after receiving that word, while in Kansas City, I was hearing a talk by Kevin Matthews, then leader of healing ministries at the International House of Prayer. Out of the blue, he mentioned that he had produced a series of tapes outlining what he believed was God's plan in the near future—to produce end-time cities of refuge. My heart leaped, as I began to realize that God had been speaking this idea to others. I purchased a set of his teachings from the Friends of the Bridegroom bookstore.

Three months later, I was attending a conference arranged by Doug Small, southeast representative for International Renewal Ministries that leads Prayer Summits in cities throughout the world. Doug was gathering people from the Southeast region of the country who were involved in building the city-wide church concept in their cities. I met many pastors and ministry leaders who, like myself, had just left local church pastorates with a calling from God on their lives to build prayer and unity among Christians in cities like Miami, Birmingham, Tuscaloosa and Charlotte.

One of the speakers was my friend, Tom White. Tom was teaching on city-wide church movements all around the world. During a private conversation, I mentioned that I had received a strong word that God wanted to make Richmond a city of refuge, but I was unsure of what it meant. His eyes widened, and he said, "No kidding. Cities of Refuge is what I am about to teach on next hour." Tom had received the same word from God for cities all around the world. When I told him about Kevin Matthews, he said, "I need to find out what this man is saying about this"—and he got from me the web-site where he could order Kevin's teaching.

Here is another of those instances where God is saying the same thing simultaneously to people in different cities, and even different countries. All of us are just trying to hear God the best we can.

Preparing Richmond

What God is doing globally must and will affect Richmond, Virginia. What is coming in the near future is going to require us to be alert to coming changes in our destiny. We must not assume that life is going to continue as it has. We must gear up the Church at Richmond to adapt to a great awakening, and to the possibility of persecution or catastrophe that will likely follow on its heels. We must try to discern what might be required of us in building a Gateway, a Bridge, and a City of Refuge.

One thing seems certain: the models of ministry and structure that we are used to will not be adequate; we must allow God to instruct us in the creation of new love relationships and new ways of ministry to meet the needs of broken people desperate for healing and for God. Above all, we must seek His presence, which has been quite rare in the streets of Richmond. We must look to the future, not the past.

What I have written above does not require us to believe in some new theory of the end-times. It only adds a note of urgency for us to get busy and do what Christ has told us to do all along. For example, in my book *The Church at Richmond*, I made a case for a city-wide church, that there are not 800 churches in Richmond, but only one. God wants to take congregations, denominations and ministries that have been separate for years, and bring them together, to put ligaments, flesh and skin on dry, separate bones. He wants the Church to be more unified than it has ever been, to learn how to love each other, trust each other and work together across racial and denominational lines.

> *Who then is the faithful and wise servant,*
> *whom the master has put in charge of the servants*
> *in his household to give them their food at the*
> *proper time? It will be good for that servant*
> *whose master finds him doing so when he returns.*
> *(Mt. 24:45-56)*

■ ■ ■

Part Four

HOW DO WE REALLY
FEEL ABOUT THE
POWER OF GOD?

Chapter Eighteen

ARE WE READY
FOR HIS PRESENCE?

It seemed right to add one more section to this book, dealing with the very real issue of whether we want God to pour out His Spirit in our midst. Even the Church has seemed to have little stomach for this today. Our country's values, priorities and world-view have shifted dramatically since the great awakenings I have described in the pages above. In fact, our entire culture has more or less abandoned the power of God as a working hypothesis, a real force at the center of all of life that drives everything.

The very concept of a great awakening seems foreign to us today. Most people, even Christians, do not really believe what the apostle Paul clearly did believe—that the Church in every city is the key to the transformation of that city. How many Americans put much stock in these promises? As Eugene Peterson puts Ephesians 1:22-23:

*He (Jesus) is in charge of it all, has the final word
on everything. At the center of all this, Christ
rules the church. The church, you see, is not
peripheral to the world; the world is peripheral to
the church. The church is Christ's body, in which
he speaks and acts, by which he fills everything
with his presence. (*The Message)*

What is needed in this kind of scenario is not bold
plans, but a keenness to see and hear God, to sense what
the Spirit is saying to the churches today. We do not, at
first, need more plans. We need eye salve to see God as
Jesus saw Him, to do nothing but what we see the Father
doing. We do not, at first, need more money. We need the
riches of Christ where moths and rust do not destroy. We
do not, at first, need to assert the trappings of our
particular racial or denominational culture, but to clothe
ourselves with Christlike humility and love.

Adjusting to the Loss of Control

Historically, Christian people have been equally upset
by moves of Satan and moves of God. Both have caused
terrible fighting among Christian people.

Why? What do these two seasons have in common?

Both are intrusions into our comfortable and well-
ordered lives. Both seem like unwelcome invasions of our
personal lives, when we cannot always have it our way and
control our churches and our cities. Both challenge us to
trust God more than we trust ourselves and our own

initiatives. Supernatural interference with our routines in the Church can meet with surprising resistance, even when God is behind them, as the apostle Peter discovered in the precincts of the Sanhedrin. (See Acts 4.)

Yet even the tempered caution of the Pharisee Gamaliel during the first Christian Revival has been rare among Christians. Gamaliel advised them: "Leave these men alone! Let them go! For if their purpose or activity is of human origin, it will fail. But if it is from God, you will not be able to stop these men" (Ac. 5:38b-39). By contrast, Christians in the West tend to oppose anything we didn't think of, and that we are not in charge of. The fear of losing control can rear its head just when we least expect it.

Christians Persecuting Christians

Moves of Satan (that is, of persecution and opposition to the gospel) can provoke very unpleasant and divisive behavior among Christians. Since we will likely have to confront this in the future, it is well for us to take a look at what has happened among Christians in past generations, and be forewarned.

In China, God provided for an indigenous Chinese Church during the 1920's and '30's, as described in the book *Against the Tide*, the biography of Watchman Nee. Through the Little Flock movement, God built a structure of house churches under the guidance of pastor Nee, a very influential Chinese leader. These structures were at variance with established Western ideas of what churches should look like.

In addition, Watchman Nee preached a strong message that Christians are not only saved for eternity, but also saved *out of the world*, the world system that is at enmity with God. As Watchman Nee was faithful to prepare the Chinese Church for what was coming (a great awakening in China, followed by satanic counterattack), he attempted to build bridges with the older established mainline denominations. He did not have a spirit of competition or pride against the Western churches that had first planted the gospel in China.

But despite many attempts by Pastor Nee to build bridges with the mainline denominations, many Western missionaries refused to honor or recognize the Little Flock movement. They did not appreciate the need for house churches, and were welded to concepts of "church" and "ministry" rooted in Western traditions.

Finally, Communism took over and the persecutions began. Communist authorities took the approach of inviting Christians in one denomination to accuse Christians in other denominations. Western Christians were more than eager to accuse Little Flock Christians in front of Communist tribunals. Little did they realize that they were playing into the hands of satanic schemes to destroy the Church. Western Christians by and large did not have a place for a personal devil in their world-view. Many saw the Little Flock as mere competitor congregations. In the end, the Communist government simply destroyed the Western-style churches when it had finished using them.

What thrives in China today is the house church movement, which learned to resist the temptation to accuse fellow believers in a Communist court. They recognized who their true enemy was and remained loyal to each other. Because they held to scriptural paradigms, they resisted satanic schemes to divide and conquer the Church.

Can We Resist Divisive Behavior?

In America, it takes very little to get us Christians to accuse one another in public settings. American preachers attack other Christian preachers, chopping up theologies and teachings as though their livelihood depended on this sort of behavior. Christians carelessly ignore scriptural counsel about how to exercise discipline or confront inappropriate behavior as delineated in Matthew 18. We write books and preach all sorts of things against each other without communicating directly with the people we are slandering or accusing or correcting.

In my reading of history, great awakenings can give rise to just as much bickering and animosity among Christians as seasons of persecution. I write this in the hope that we will be cautious about critical and destructive words toward those who believe and behave differently from ourselves during a season of awakening. There are many different Christian cultures in Richmond. Each has validity. Each has its weaknesses. There is a pearl of God ensconced in the midst of each. Are we willing to look for the pearls, and zip our lip when it comes to pointing out the weaknesses of the other traditions, until God is really calling us to do so.[2]

Ruth Ruibal's book, *Unity in the Spirit*, is a masterful account of the temptations that beset Christian leaders in the midst of a spiritual awakening—temptations to criticize, to hold on to offenses, to destroy what God is doing because we want to control it, or because we choose to indulge in the luxury of bitterness.

If Richmond is to become a city of refuge, Christians must finally get wise to satanic strategies and resist them. He is behind the spirit of domination and control, and he is more clever than we realize. We cannot outwit him with our minds. But by clinging humbly to Christ, we can overcome him, and he will become like ashes under our feet.

■ ■ ■

Chapter Nineteen

CONFUSION REIGNS

George Otis, who knows as much as anyone about spiritual awakenings around the globe today, says that the West is the only place around the world where there is little or no evidence of true transformation by the power of God. At the time of this writing, he finds several hundred communities where He sees this transformation of cities because of the prayers of Christian people clinging to the promises of God. The lack of this in Western countries speaks volumes about our spirituality—and the state of our faith.

This final section is an attempt to address this problem nationally, because national trends do affect us. Richmond is a part of America, and America is part of the Western world. What is it about the West that has so closed us to the power of God—even when we see manifestations of

God's power elsewhere around the globe? Why are we now seemingly so closed off from God?

Faith in God's Power

Today, most Americans do not know what to believe about the power of God. In other countries, this confusion is not so widespread. Most Christians in Third World countries believe in God's power, and that is why they pray. In Africa, it is easy to get whole stadiums full of people to pray. A Ghanaian pastor recently described to me how Ghanaian Christians go into the woods and pray all night long.

Most Americans would doubt the value of such an investment in prayer. Because God's power depends on prayer, our unbelief feeds in on itself, confirming every day how right we are not to believe that God will do much of anything in this world of natural law.

The American Fascination for Programs

It is common for us Americans to go to church, recite Christian doctrines, do Christian ministries and even pray a bit, yet without a scrap of faith in the power of God for today.

A friend of mine, Brad Long, tells the following story from his many years as a missionary in Taiwan. One day, a denominational executive from the U.S. visiting Taiwan held a conference on evangelism. During the conference he asked the pastors what program they used to accomplish evangelism in their cities. They replied, "We pray. The people are converted. They come to the church. We baptize them and they become members."

The executive responded, "No, no. That is not what I am asking. I want to know what *program* you are using to accomplish evangelism."

The pastors looked at one another, wondering if there was a problem with translation. They repeated, "We pray. The people are converted. They come to church. We baptize them and they become members."

The American stared blankly at them, wondering, too, whether there wasn't some problem with translation, so he stated his question again more succinctly. "What program…"

There was a disconnect there, you see, created not by a language barrier, but by a difference of world-view. To the Chinese, the only "program" worth talking about was God's program: prayer. The Chinese understood that prayer draws the power of God, and God alone can convert hearts. No one comes to Christ unless the Father draws him.

But to the American, prayer was not relevant. Sure, Christians should pray. Who would ever speak against prayer? But it is programs invented by church executives that will get the job done, or so we think. Programs are everything for Americans, because we believe that the world will be won to Christ by our ingenuity. If the first ten programs fail to produce expected results, we keep on searching, because we really feel that the failure is due to a lack of ingenuity on our part.

Look deeper. Our belief in programs rises out of the fact that we believe a good deal more in our own power than in God's.

When Your World-view Is Offended

Some of us might say, "Yes, but if God would just *do* something for us, it would be easier to believe in His power, and it would be easier to invest more time in prayer."

It is not as simple as that. Let me tell the story of another friend, Delores Winder. Delores grew up in Louisiana and was a member of a mainline denominational church. In 1956, she was diagnosed with a deadly disease for which there was no cure.

My illness began in 1956 and in January of the next year the surgeons performed the first spinal fusion using bone grafts from the tibia to hold my vertebrae in place. They took bone for the fusion from the larger of the two bones of my leg–between the knee and ankle–and fused it with my vertebrae.

The doctors called my illness pseudo-arthrosis and told me there was no known cure for stopping it or even controlling it. The only alternative was to live and die with it.

They explained to me that an ordinary
person's blood stream contains everything
necessary to keep a person's bones healthy.
But someone like me, with pseudo-arthrosis,
is different. My bones refused to absorb what
they needed from the blood stream so my
bones became dry and brittle, and I developed
advanced, acute osteoporosis causing the bones
to age much before their time.[1]

Because Delores was in constant severe pain from this disease, the doctors performed on her a percutaneous cordotomy, a surgical procedure reserved for terminal patients, in which the nerve centers at the base of the brain are burned out. She also had to wear a body cast just to be able to move around.

One day, she was persuaded, out of sheer desperation and the persistence of a neighbor, to attend a Kathryn Kuhlman healing service. At that service, she was dramatically healed by the power of God. In a single day, God gave her a new body and a whole new lease on life. Her nerve centers were restored, her back was healed. She was literally given a new body.

She returned to her church that Sunday expecting to hear an announcement from the pulpit about her wonderful healing. Yet no announcement was made. Soon it became clear: her healing was an embarrassment to her church. Her church friends, who had known her for years, were embarrassed by the *way* in which she had been healed. If it had been through a doctor, working through medical science, they would have rejoiced, sure enough. But because she had been healed by the power of God, they considered her a freak and an anomaly. Eventually, Delores had to leave her church. The people could not cope with her healing. It was too threatening to their most basic assumptions about how the world goes.

Have We All Become Deists?

Most Americans hover around the edges of deism. Deists believe in God, but they do not believe that God will do anything for us today. They believe only that God was present at Creation to establish moral and natural laws.

Every year, I hear someone reiterate the notion that the Founding Fathers of our country were mostly deists. This is a good example of how present-day world-views try to re-shape the past to fit with present opinion.

John Eidsmoe dealt with this issue thoroughly in his excellent book, *Christianity and the Constitution*. He wrote:

> *The colonists were familiar with deist thinking. But deism never gained a strong foothold in America. The first Great Awakening, the religious revival of the 1740's, was partially responsible for cutting short the spread of deism.*
>
> *In many states at the time of the Constitutional Convention, confessed deists were not allowed to*

hold public office. Deism was generally held in low esteem, as such laws indicate.[2]

Eidsmoe then sets forth the research of Dr. M. E. Bradford of the University of Dallas, from which he concludes that only three out of 55 signers of the Constitution were known deists: Benjamin Franklin, James Wilson and Hugh Williamson. *Christianity and the Constitution* goes on to look at the true beliefs of founders like George Washington, Thomas Jefferson and James Madison, based on personal letters and church membership.

Back in the Olden Days

Today, however, Americans prefer to believe that our founders *were* deists and we have maintained a studied ignorance of the great awakenings of the past. I remember years ago reading the word *awakening* in some old Presbyterian documents, and I thought, "I wonder what that is? Some quaint old expression they used back in the olden days, I guess." It has taken some considerable effort to force my way past this wall of cultural fog and discover what really happened by God's power in our own collective past.

A Spiritual Void

The lack of prayer-leading-to-awakening has left a massive spiritual hunger among all those churches that have learned to rely on human ingenuity. People and denominations that have cut themselves off from the true power of God sooner or later will turn to other spiritual sources.

I look back to my own seminary experience. In my first year of seminary, leaders on campus invited Timothy Leary, the drug guru and LSD advocate to address seminary students. Leary believed that LSD was the best pathway to God.

Later, my seminary established a department of spiritual studies to try to address the lack of spirituality during the '70's. Dr. Morton Kelsey became adjunct professor of the department, and I attended the opening convocation. Kelsey quoted from Carl Jung more than any other writer. He considered Jung the highest twentieth-century authority on spiritual matters. Many of the exercises of spirituality promoted at that convocation seemed to have Buddha, not Jesus, as their inspiration.

More recently still, my seminary hosted a speaker known for developing goddess feminism in a "Christian" context. This woman actually tried to erect an Asherah pole at her theological institution.

These disturbing trends show the profound confusion that reigns among many groups of Christians about spiritual power. Modernism, the belief in science as the sole arbiter of truth, has yielded to post-modernism, the belief that there is no arbiter of truth at all. Much of the church is going right along with this trend.

It is sometimes difficult for Christians to swim against the tide. The prevailing world-view in a culture is like water that surrounds you. It comes at you everywhere, and it is hard to resist its influence.

However, if we are about to enter a season when God will stage a major re-entry into our culture, then it is a good time to remind ourselves that LSD, Buddhism and Asherah poles do not lead us to the power of God. Christian people have no business sniffing up those trees. It is time to rediscover our faith in God and God's power. To help us evaluate this direction, let me do a little spiritual mapping of Western culture, because that culture does affect us all.

■ ■ ■

Chapter Twenty

WHAT HAPPENED TO GOD'S POWER?

Most people still think of America as a Christian nation. Most people in other countries maintain this impression, and most Christians like to cling to it, too.

Yet few of us seem to be aware that a century ago, the majority of Americans passed through a transition that placed serious doubt around the whole idea of trusting God's power for anything. This dramatic change began in Europe and, spreading to the U.S., affected our educational system. It explains why most Western nations are slow to participate in the worldwide awakening to God's power typified in the Cali and Cape Town experiences.

The Transformation of Our Schools

Prior to the 20th century, the power of God was an important, even central, issue for many Christians. Many Americans had been deeply touched by God during one of several seasons of spiritual awakening, as I have described. Our oldest schools were established during the Great Awakening, including our Ivy League schools and our first theological seminary at Princeton. Our public school system was an outgrowth of the Second Great Awakening, awash in the power of God. People of those eras were deeply aware of God's power and they talked a good deal about how to invite and respond to spiritual awakenings.

In his book, *Revival and Revivalism*, Iain Murray describes the ongoing debate between Calvinists and Arminians during those years of spiritual awakening. Their debate focused on the issue of how to make sure that we retain God's power in American life. So they asked: Does God pour out His power during these seasons just because He wants to? (It's just predestined, that's all.) Or is there some part we play in His decisions? (We hear and respond to His covenant promises, then He pours out His power.)

Most of the early Christians in our country were Calvinists, who believed that God just decided these things. Gradually, the emphasis shifted toward the human element, until Charles Finney, in the 1830's, insisted that anyone can have "Revival" if they are willing to pay the price and do what God says. It is not my purpose to take a position on the Calvinism-Arminianism issue, but to point out that the power of God was a significant part of people's lives, and that is why they talked about it.

God's Power to Awaken People to Jesus

Since the very concept of *the power of God* has vanished from our public life, and it is often a rather vague concept today, perhaps it would be helpful to include some examples of what those "awakened" Christians meant by it. Few of us have any conception of a great awakening—how the power and majesty of God can settle into a town or city, so that everyone in that place has to deal with His Majesty.

A few descriptions will show that these past generations were not dealing with theories and doctrines studied in their library carels, but with the reality of Jesus Christ that had marched right into their lives and confronted them with true authority and power. Their discussions were based on encounters with God not theological textbooks.

Here, for example, is a glimpse from Jonathan Edwards into the very beginning of the Great Awakening in Northampton, Massachusetts. It was written at the time of the events he describes, 1735, so there is no room for poor memory or exaggeration:

> *There was scarcely a single person in the town, either old or young, that was left unconcerned about the great things of the eternal world. Those that were wont to be the vainest and loosest, and those that had been most disposed to think and*

*speak slightly of vital and experimental religion,
were now generally subject to great awakenings.
And the work of conversion was carried on in a
most astonishing manner, and increased more and
more; souls did, as it were, come by flocks to
Jesus Christ. ...*

*This work of God, as it was carried on, and
the number of true saints multiplied, soon made a
glorious alteration in the town; so that in the
spring and summer following, anno 1735, the
town seemed to be full of the presence of God; it
never was so full of love, nor so full of joy, and
yet so full of distress as it was then. There were
remarkable tokens of God's presence in almost
every house.*[1]

What we see is that when Jesus comes, he can
sometimes impose himself on whole communities.
Because people are confronted with the reality of Him,
they are forced to make a decision about Him on the spot.
No yawns. No religious debates. The Kingdom of God
comes when the King Himself comes. And it is impossible
to be neutral about Him.

David Brainerd

People of European background are not the only ones
who can experience the power of God. Christianity is not
the white man's religion. Here is another example of the
power of God from the pen of David Brainerd, who
preached among Native people in New Jersey in 1745:

...The power of God seemed to descend upon the assembly "like a rushing mighty wind," and with an astonishing energy bore down all before it.

I stood amazed at the influence that seized the audience almost universally, and could compare it to nothing more aptly than the irresistible force of a mighty torrent, or swelling deluge that with its insupportable weight and pressure bears down and sweeps before it whatever is in its way. Almost all persons of all ages were bowed down with concern together and scarce one was able to withstand the shock of this surprising operation. Old men and women, who had been drunken wretches for many years, and some little children, not more than six or seven years of age, appeared in distress for their souls, as well as persons of middle age.

...The most stubborn hearts were now obliged to bow. A principal man among the Indians, who before was most secure and self-righteous and thought his state good because he knew more than the generality of the Indians had formerly done, and who with a great degree of confidence the day before, told me, "he had been a Christian more than ten years," was now brought under solemn concern for his soul and wept bitterly.

...Some of the white people who came out of curiosity to "hear what this babbler would say"

to the poor ignorant Indians were much awakened, and some appeared to be wounded with a view of their perishing state.

Those who had lately obtained relief were filled with comfort at this season. They appeared calm and composed, and seemed to rejoice in Christ Jesus.

There was one remarkable instance of awakening this day that I cannot but take particular notice of here. A young Indian woman, who, I believe, never knew before she had a soul nor ever thought of any such thing, hearing that there was something strange among the Indians, came to see what was the matter. On her way to the Indians she called at my lodgings, and when I told her I designed presently to preach to the Indians, laughed, and seemed to mock; but went, however, to them.

I had not proceeded far in my public discourse, before she felt effectually that she had a soul. Before I had concluded my discourse, she was so convinced of her sin and misery and so distressed with concern for her soul's salvation that she seemed like one pierced through with a dart, and cried out incessantly. She could neither go nor stand, nor sit on her seat without being held up. After public service was over, she lay flat on the ground praying earnestly, and would take no notice of, nor give any answer to any that spoke to her. I hearkened to know what she said,

and perceived the burden of her prayer to be ...
"Have mercy on me, and help me to give
You my heart." Thus she continued praying
incessantly for many hours together. This was
indeed a surprising day of God's power and
seemed enough to convince an atheist of the
truth, importance and power of God's Word.[2]

Some may wonder about the amount of weeping over "sin and misery" in these accounts. Isn't God a God of love? Why are people so deeply serious in these accounts, actually crying out in fear and desperation?

Certainly the love of Jesus shines through these stories, but when Jesus presents Himself as King of the Universe, we become aware of a righteousness that not only loves and accepts us, but also makes demands on us to behave in the ways of love ourselves. Here is where we are caught up short, are convicted of sin, the failure to love. We become aware of the awesomeness of God's love, all right. But when it stands up next to us, we also become aware of our selfishness and the false motives in even our most loving deeds. Let's call this "severe mercy."

Charles Finney

Here is another account from a century later—Charles Finney's evangelistic ministry at Rome, New York. This shows how Jesus can take over whole communities, confronting them with His presence and power:

The state of things in the village and in the
surrounding area was such that no one could

come into the village without feeling awestricken with the impression that God was there in a peculiar and wonderful way. As an example of this I will relate a particular incident. The sheriff of the county resided in Utica. There were two courthouses in the county, one in Rome and the other at Utica. Consequently, the sheriff, Bryant by name, came to Rome quite frequently. He later told me that he had heard of the state of things at Rome, and he, together with many others in Utica, had laughed a great deal about it.

But one day it was necessary for him to come to Rome. He said that he was glad to have business there, for he wanted to see for himself what things were really like. He was driving in his one-horse sleigh without any particular impression in his mind at all, until he crossed what was called the old canal, a place about a mile from the town. He said as soon as he crossed the canal, a strange impression came over him, an awe so deep that he could not shake it. He felt as if God permeated the whole atmosphere. He said that this feeling increased the whole way, until he came into the village. He stopped at Mr. Franklin's hotel, and the stable-man looked just like he himself felt—as if he were afraid to speak. He went into the hotel and found the gentleman there with whom he had business. He said that they were both so obviously shaken that they could hardly attend to business. He reported that several times in the course of the short time he was there, he had to rise from the table abruptly and go to the window and look away, trying to divert his attention to keep from weeping. He saw that everyone else appeared to feel just as he did. Such an awe, such a solemness, such a state of things he had never had any conception of before. He quickly concluded his business and returned to Utica—but (as he said later) never to speak lightly of the work at Rome again. And a few weeks later in Utica, he himself became converted.[3]

Stories like these were a part of our American collective experience 150 years ago. Today they are forgotten, except to a few.

Looking back on my own experience as a student in the '60's, I cannot remember a single instance when I was told of these great awakenings, not even in church. The amnesia was so complete that nothing but a blank space remained. We Americans more or less agreed: "That was then, and this is now."

This feels like an enormous loss. It is as though we thought the power of God was unworthy of remembrance. Let me trace this development in our spiritual life together.

■ ■ ■

Chapter Twenty-one

FAIR WARNING
A HUNDRED YEARS AGO

I have said that the abandonment of the power of God came from our institutions of learning. Let us examine how this happened. One day, William James, professor of philosophy at Harvard University, became so profoundly concerned about the whole trend of Western culture and higher learning that he trekked across the Atlantic Ocean to deliver a series of lectures at Edinburgh University, the famed Gifford lectures. These were perhaps the most famous lectures of the century, delivered in 1902 by one of the greatest intellects we have produced.

Today, these lectures, published under the title, *The Varieties of Religious Experience*, are considered a classic. I saw the book recently at the bookstore among other great classics still considered hot items.

God at the Heart of All Philosophy

William James was trying to tell a skeptical audience of Europeans that the foundational insight of Western thought has always been: *We need God*. In his own words:

There is a state of mind, known to religious men, but to no others, in which the will to assert ourselves and hold our own has been displaced by a willingness to close our mouths and be as nothing in the floods and waterspouts of God. In this state of mind, what we most dreaded has become the habitation of our safety, and the hour of our moral death has turned into our spiritual birthday. The time for tension in our soul is over, and that of happy relaxation, of calm deep breathing, of an eternal present, with no discordant future to be anxious about, has arrived. Fear is not held in abeyance as it is by mere mortality, it is positively expunged and washed away. ...Religious feeling is thus an absolute addition to the Subject's range of life. It gives him a new sphere of power. When the outward battle is lost, and the outer world disowns him, it redeems and vivifies an interior world which otherwise would be an empty waste.[1]

Through six lectures, William James underscored the need for us all to surrender our lives to God. Lecture by lecture, he described first the reality of the unseen world, then the sickness of all human souls, the necessity of conversion if our sick souls will be healed, and the importance of saintliness (sanctification) by the power of God. Through it all, James needled his hearers with the futility of all the current alternatives that intellectuals were toying with, answers to human woes that flow from human cleverness and optimism.

He especially stressed (in two lectures) the importance and necessity of conversion if we are to have any peace at all, and he gave dozens of instances from every conceivable Christian tradition to show that this is so: from the Russian Orthodox Leo Tolstoy, to the evangelical George Muller, to the American theologian Jonathan Edwards, to the revivalist Charles Finney, to Billy Bray ("an illiterate English evangelist"), to Father Vianney ("a French country priest"). He also retold the stories of a host of others you and I have never heard of, but who had in their own simple way known God's power to change hearts.

William James still used words like "soul," "spiritual birthday," "conversion" and "floods of God." He was the last major American thinker to do so, and the last to draw heavily upon the great awakenings and "revivals" of our past. He warned that each denominational tradition tends to limit God to its own experience of Him—leading to triteness and narrowness. Nevertheless, he validated this whole dimension of our history. Awakenings. The power of God to convert hearts.

By contrast, he regarded our confidence in science and the rational mind as a shallow optimism that has never been justified by experience. He added that it takes more than a shallow faith in rational science (whatever the current cosmogony—he especially singled out the theory of evolution) to deal with the kind of evil we have in this world. He harped on this theme repeatedly, and got away with it because he was so highly respected.

At the heart of his lectures, he warned that the evil residing in the world will not be overcome by mere optimism or human science: "The normal process of life contains moments as bad as any of those which insane melancholy is filled with, moments in which radical evil gets its innings and takes its solid turn."[2]

A Stern Warning

Very seldom has anyone in the history of our country delivered a more serious and straightforward warning to whole nations. Seldom has anyone laid out the choices or conveyed the dangers he saw waiting to engulf the Western world in the twentieth century.

But William James saw an ominous trend, the very trend I am pointing out here. Westerners were becoming fascinated with seemingly new possibilities. We were becoming confident in ourselves, ready to take matters into our own hands. It was as though we were building a geodesic dome, a glass structure that glassed God out, while turning all of life into one huge scientific experiment. In this brave new world, God became an unwelcome subject for public conversation especially in academic circles. As

William James concluded his lectures, he said, "The current of thought in academic circles runs against me, and I feel like a man who must set his back against an open door quickly if he does not wish to see it closed and locked."[3]

Perhaps that is why he trekked to Edinburgh in the first place (becoming the first of our great thinkers to do so). He saw that Western thought was rejecting the power of God as a necessary element in coping with evil. To that extent, he saw Europe moving into a dangerous dead end road, a road that it did, in fact, explore to the bitter end during the rest of the century.

William James, like Jeremiah, had the unenviable task of delivering a warning to a whole continent full of people who refused to hear what he had to say. In time, as I will show, American culture followed the trend, and then the American Church followed the culture.

■ ■ ■

Chapter Twenty-two

A RESPONSE FROM EUROPE

I t seems unlikely that William James ever got to know
Sigmund Freud personally. Freud gets no more than
honorable mention in William James's lectures.
However, if anyone had the intelligence and stature to
answer William James, it was Freud, the psychiatrist from
Vienna. And he did.

Freud, like James, had one foot in the study of the
psyche, and the other in philosophy. He wrote a book, *The
Future of an Illusion*, in which he stated his own philosophy.
It was just exactly what William James warned against.

Glassing God Out of Our World

If William James continued to use words like "soul,"
"conversion" and "spiritual birthday," Freud went to

great lengths to rid himself of all such words. He wanted to study human problems in a truly scientific way, and his world-view had no place for a spiritual realm. So much for William James's lecture on "The Reality of the Unseen."

A case in point: for centuries, the inner sense of right and wrong called conscience had been treated as a reflection of our spiritual nature, an evidence of the existence of God. (C.S. Lewis, writing later, treated it this way in *Mere Christianity*.) But Freud re-named the conscience "superego." *Superego* is a creative word designed to replace traditional words because traditional words have supernatural, spiritual overtones. They imply the existence of God and a human spirit, and Freud wanted to rid himself of all such hocus-pocus. Freud did not believe that the inner sense of right and wrong reflected the nature of God at all. To him, the superego was nothing but a mental repository of morals left over from early childhood training.

Behind this approach to healing the human soul there grew up a new approach to all human problems. Freud wanted to apply Enlightenment principles to what had been called the cure of souls, so that we could make advancements in observation, method and knowledge and solve every human problem scientifically.

He wrote: "We believe that it is possible for scientific work to discover something about the reality of the world through which we can increase our power and according to which we can regulate our life."[1]

Freud was not alone in believing that science was a new answer to all human problems. But he was one of the boldest in expressing this great European hope:

> *The scientific spirit engenders a particular attitude to the problems of this world; before the problems of religion it halts for a while, then wavers, and finally here too steps over the threshold. In this process there is no stopping. The more the fruits of knowledge become accessible to men, the more widespread is the decline of religious belief, at first only of the obsolete and objectionable expressions of the same, then of its fundamental assumptions also.*[2]

To Freud, religious faith was an unproved assumption, therefore an "illusion," which must inevitably fall before the steady march of scientific method. The scholarly institutions of Europe took up the challenge of gaining "the fruits of knowledge" and in so doing abandoned their own historic experience with the power of God. Intellectuals forgot the issues of world-view raised by William James and assumed that the new leaders of Europe were correct in these new directions. They came to believe that the human race *has* discovered a new method of overcoming all problems. The new method is: Method. Scientific method.

Freud and his generation were defending what they considered a new world-view and a new hope. That world-view was to be built not around the power of God, but around the power of the rational mind.

My Search for God

Let me demonstrate how all-pervasive this change became in this country even in theological schools by mid-century.

As a teenager and later as an art student during the '60's, I began to sense the presence of God in my life, through the beauty of the world God had made. My spirit was awakening to God's Spirit, and I wanted to know Him better. Also, I had been studying the Bible in my Presbyterian youth group, and I was sensing (in my spirit) that God had much to tell me here. So I decided to get to know God.

If God is worth knowing, I reasoned, I ought to devote several years of my life to discovering Him. So I entered seminary. I naively believed that in seminary I would get to know God better, because a seminary is a *theological* place, a place for the study of God.

In the '60's, however, seminaries were not designed to help people know God. Our classes in Bible study dealt entirely with "higher criticism of the Bible." Higher criticism of the Bible is our attempt to treat the Bible scientifically. Through scientific method, you decide whether Moses really did or did not write the first five books of the Bible, or whether 2 Peter was really written by Peter. The disciplines of higher criticism had virtually taken over Bible study classes.

William Tyndale had never translated the Bible into English for this purpose. Tyndale, who had an evangelist's heart, was interested in helping people follow Jesus. He was so gripped by his work of translation that he literally sacrificed his life to put the English Bible into people's hands. But at my seminary, in the '60's, William Tyndale was never mentioned, and the Bible was not treated as the sword of the Spirit to cut at our hearts. Instead, we were using the scalpel of scientific inquiry to dissect the Bible.

Something in me was deeply disappointed by this scientific approach to the Bible. During my four years in seminary, my heart was crying out: "No–o–o. This can't be right. This is not what the Bible is for. This is not helping me know God better."

But this was what they were doing in theological seminaries in those days. They were not studying God. Nor were they any longer involved in ways to help people find Jesus through the power of God's word. They were trying to demonstrate the triumph of science. Perhaps they felt that this approach was necessary to be relevant to a culture that had all but abandoned the power of God revealed in the Bible. It was part of a massive scientific project that spread out into all of our institutions of learning, even seminaries.

My spiritual hunger for God, I began to realize, would have to wait. The whole of Western culture was working on a separate project, the one that Sigmund Freud had described. We were exploring a different power source than the power of God. We were into the rational mind now, and we had to learn how to scientifically dissect Holy Writ along with everything else.

What Power Source Do We Ultimately Trust?

This was nothing other than what Sigmund Freud had announced from Vienna. "We believe that it is possible for scientific work to discover something about the reality of the world through which we can increase *our power*," Freud had written, expressing the hopes of his generation. Quite a change from the thinking of William James, who had said that conversion adds "a whole new sphere of power" to a person's life. William James had been speaking of the power of God.

Because the West was turning away from God's power, it was no longer interested in spiritual awakening. We wanted to discover and build our lives around another source of power, and we were consumed with excitement over the whole project.

The Force of a World-view

Perhaps it would be helpful to say a word about world-views here. World-views are like the operating system on your computer. Most of us don't pay attention to our operating systems. We mainly think about the new software packages that we can buy and use on top of the operating system. Few of us ever study operating systems. We just accept the operating system that comes with the computer.

In the same way, few of us delve down into our world-view to examine how it works. Most of us take the world-view that was given to us, and we just use it without questioning it. Few of us like to take time and energy to examine our world-view, let alone to change over to a completely different one. Changing a world-view is very inconvenient. We have to learn to think and walk through life differently than we learned at first. Most people don't do this unless they are converted by God or move to another country.

Years ago, computer designers developed DOS as an operating system. Then Windows was developed and became popular because it was judged to be more powerful and useful than DOS. When I went from DOS to Windows, it took quite some doing to learn how the new operating system worked. It would have been easier just to keep using DOS. But people said that Windows was better, so I decided to make the change. I bought a computer with Windows on it, and learned how to use it.

That is what was happening in the West a hundred years ago. We were going to a new operating system that was being judged better—more powerful and useful. But instead of changing from DOS to Windows, we went from Windows to DOS, because DOS was judged better. DOS is the Doubter's Operating System, because it is based on the ability to doubt everything until proven true. Windows offered us windows into the heavenly realm where God is, and it was judged to be obsolete.

The Power Question at the Heart of Every World-view

World-views are built around power sources. A world-view answers the question, "Where does the power come from to live life successfully?" So far, we have looked at two answers to that question: from God, and from our own rational minds. (There is a third possible power source that has become popular more recently, and I deal with that in the next two chapters.)

Many intellectuals at the turn of the last century were convinced that they had discovered a new rational source of power: scientific method. Scientific method has indeed proven to be very powerful. But it does not have the power Freud thought it had. It does not have the power to heal our broken hearts.

Also, the world-view they were trying out was not new. It had been discovered centuries before and had already been discarded by the man who, more than any other single person, shaped Western thought and made it Christian.

His name was Augustine, and I will tell of him in the next chapter. It is important to recognize why Western thought retained a basic faith in the power of God for so many centuries. Its reasons, I believe, were good ones. The West followed Augustine's Christian lead for reasons that are still valid. The reasons for abandoning the power of God, in my judgment, were not valid at all, and are still not valid.

Augustine, long before William James, had found some serious problems with the DOS operating system, the one based on scientific method. But very few people in the twentieth century were interested in heeding warnings, whether new warnings from William James, or old warnings from Augustine.

We just wanted to be left alone to work on our project.

■ ■ ■

Chapter Twenty-three

AUGUSTINE ESTABLISHES THE CHRISTIAN WEST

Many people know that the West became "Christian" when Constantine was converted to Christ in 312 A.D.

In reality, though, no one is really converted to Christ just because their emperor is converted. It was another man, sixty-six years later, who won the hearts and minds of most Romans to the lordship of Christ. That man was Augustine, who was converted 74 years after Constantine, in 386 A.D.

Augustine wrote two books that deeply influenced the Roman Empire and Europe (by extension) for centuries to come. As a matter of fact, the writers of the Protestant Reformation a dozen centuries later quoted Augustine almost as much as they quoted the apostle Paul. Augustine published his *Confessions* in 400 A.D, then wrote *The City of God* as a series of articles between 413 and 426. These two books were a spiritual infusion that convinced most Romans to believe in the power of God, and to build their world-view around that source of power.

Augustine Explores His World-view Options

You can trace Augustine's search for a viable operating system by reading the first nine chapters of *Confessions*.

Augustine started out as a simple pagan. True, his mother was a Christian and tried to get him to read his Bible and go to church, but he didn't want to do any of these things. Instead, he decided to explore Manichaean faith.

Manichaeism was the religious system founded by Mani, a Babylonian who declared himself to be the last great prophet after Adam, Zoroaster, the Buddha and Jesus. Mani stands in a long line of religious leaders who have had encounters with angels who downloaded religious systems into their heads. Mohammed, the founder of Islam is an example, who said the same thing about himself that Mani did. Joseph Smith, the founder of Mormonism, is another example. Actually, there are a great many people in this category, all making claims about themselves based on "truth" downloaded by angels. The spirit that Mani encountered revealed all sorts of "truths," so Mani started a new church, "The Church of the Truth."

Claims of this sort are vastly different from the claims of Christians about Jesus Christ, that He is God Incarnate, a perfect representation of God in human form. This "incarnation" (which C. S. Lewis called "the grand miracle") paved the way for a completely unique world-view based on the salvation history that flows from the life of Jesus: that He died as an atonement for sin, ascended to the "power" position at the right hand of the Father and that He ministers by the Holy Spirit to each succeeding generation, until He returns at the end of the age. Jesus was not merely an angel, as we discover by reading the book of Hebrews, chapters 1 and 2. Colossians 1 and Ephesians 1 describe the truth about Jesus, and why His power differs markedly from the power of angels. Jesus was not just one of a long line of prophets, soon to be outshone by so-and-so, who is "the last great prophet." Encounters with angels lead to a completely different world-view based not on the power of God, but on the power of mid-level spirits. People like Mani get their power not from God, even though they may talk about God. They get their power from mid-level spirits. The same is true of Joseph Smith, and a host of others.

At any rate, Augustine started his search for a world-view as a Manichaean. After several years of searching out the "truth" of Mani, however, Augustine became somewhat jaded about this faith and the operating system on which it rested. In his own words:

So many most fabulous and absurd things were imposed to be believed, because they could not be demonstrated.[1]

Augustine was fascinated with the truth revealed by angels, but he increasingly had the feeling that he was being led around by the nose. He began to feel that there ought to be some way of checking out the truthfulness or untruthfulness of different claims. Perhaps he was feeling the frustration behind the words of that famous Roman, Pontius Pilate, "What is truth?" Many Romans were asking the same question, and Augustine's search was the search of millions. It still is.

Aristotle and the Academics

It was this inner uncertainty that thrust Augustine into an exploration of the DOS system that eventually became such a fond hope of Freud and his generation. This world-view, placing its whole confidence in the power of the rational mind, had been developed by Aristotle and was known as Academic philosophy. Aristotle wanted to develop a system of doubt and skepticism, by which, through accurate observation and scientific method, he could distinguish false from true. Augustine bought into this for a few years, "for I wished to be made just as certain of things that I could not see, as I was certain that seven and three make ten."[2]

But after a few years, Augustine began to sense that this operating system was impractical, except in a narrow range of concerns. William James later discovered this same problem with this operating system for doubters.

> ...*If we look on man's whole mental life as it exists, on the life of men that lies in them apart from their learning and science, and that they*

inwardly, and privately follow, we have to confess
that the part of it of which rationalism can give an
account is relatively superficial. It is the part that
has the prestige *undoubtedly, for it has the*
loquacity, it can challenge you for proofs, and
chop logic, and put you down with words. But it
will fail to convince or convert you all the same,
if your dumb intuitions are opposed to its
conclusions. If you have intuitions at all, they
come from a deeper level of your nature....[3]

Augustine also pointed out that it is simply impossible to check everything out rationally, even though we may fool ourselves into thinking that that is what we are doing. For example, "I thought of how I held with fixed and unassailable faith that I was born of certain parents, and this I could never know unless I believed it by hearing about them."[4] Most of the facts of life are accepted by faith. Someone tells you, and you believe them. It is impossible to avoid living by faith to some degree.

This DOS or "Enlightenment" world-view is even more impractical when we try to evaluate the spirit realm. Of course, we can pretend that the unseen realm does not exist, and that we have no spiritual nature in ourselves. But this pretending does not make the unseen realm any less real. Nor is it helpful to deny our own spiritual nature merely because it is partly hidden from scientific scrutiny.

These were the objections that Augustine ran into as he tried to make Aristotle's world-view work for himself. Having tried this, he finally concluded: "There's got to be more than this."

There was. Here is how he discovered the "more."

Augustine Experiences God's Power

Augustine had been increasingly tormented about human savagery. He was deeply disturbed about the whole trend of Roman life, which was becoming more and more depraved. Exhibit One: the blood lust of the gladiatorial arena.

He saw a close friend get sucked into attending these bloody shows, arranged for the "entertainment" of the masses. "As he saw that blood, he drank in savageness at the same time. He did not turn away, but fixed his sight on it, and drank in madness without knowing it. He took delight in that evil struggle, and he became drunk on blood and pleasure."[5] Eventually this friend was delivered of this savagery by Christ, but that was long afterwards.

Augustine wondered if all human beings were really savage creatures underneath that thin veneer of Greco-Roman civility. Is there any true "good" to be found in the human heart or in the world God made? As he looked out into Rome, he saw the seeds of its lust in himself, and he became more and more disturbed by it.

At one point, a friend of his, a simple man of ordinary giftedness, was delivered of lust by turning his life over to Christ. Augustine responded with bitterness: "The unlearned start up and 'take' heaven by force, and we with our learning, and without heart, lo, where we wallow in flesh and blood."[6] Augustine felt trapped in his own head. He became more and more desperate to find cleanness and goodness somewhere, and some sort of deliverance from the lust of the flesh, but his head wasn't helping him. One day, as he became more and more depressed about the basic human bondage in which we all seem to find ourselves, he heard a little child singing from a neighboring house, "Take up and read; take up and read."

He thought, "What sort of song is this? Why would a child sing 'take up and read?'"

Suddenly, it dawned on him that perhaps God was using a child to bring a message *to his heart*. Remembering stories his mother had told him about Christians who had experienced such leadings from God, He turned to a Bible nearby, opened it, and read the first words his eyes fell on: "…not in rioting and drunkenness, not in chambering and wantonness, not in strife and envying; but put ye on the Lord Jesus Christ, and make not provision for the flesh" (Rom. 13:13, 14). Suddenly, without warning, he felt that he was delivered from lust by the power of God's word. God's word had power to reach deep into his heart, and do what his own mind could not do.

Immediately, he reported to his mother that God had intervened in his life with power. Then they rejoiced together, for Augustine knew that his mother had been praying for him for many years with "pitiful and most sorrowful groanings."[7] Augustine spent the rest of his life building his life and his world-view around the power of God. He wrote *The City of God* to convince all of Rome that they should do the same.

Three Lessons

There are several lessons we can learn from this encounter with God, which led Augustine to a genuine conversion of heart and a complete change of world-view.

First, God must often offend our minds to convince our hearts. Augustine's learning did not and could not lead him to God. But God used a child's song to be Augustine's guide, and the philosopher had to be willing to come to God as a little child. Down through the ages God has been amazingly consistent in this way.

The apostle Paul had noticed this tendency in God: that God does not necessarily honor our maturity and intelligence. He habitually hides Himself from those who take pride in intellect: "God chose the foolish things of the world to shame the wise; God chose the weak things of the world to shame the strong. He chose the lowly things of this world and the despised things–and the things that are not–to nullify the things that are, so that no one may boast before him" (1 Cor. 1:27-29).

Paul was, in turn, borrowing from the teaching of Jesus: "I praise you, Father, Lord of heaven and earth, because you have hidden these things from the wise and learned, and revealed them to little children. Yes, Father, for this was your good pleasure" (Lk. 10:21).

Second, Augustine had to open his heart to God and learn to trust Him, even when his mind could not be certain of what he was doing. Augustine had come to a place of desperation. He was in despair about human nature, and about himself. He cried out. He came to the end of his rope. And that is where God's rope began. At that point of despair, God introduced Himself to Augustine.

God knew that He had created Augustine with a heart, not just a mind. He chose to communicate heart to heart and "deep unto deep," not mind to mind. It is not that He asked Augustine to "check his mind at the door." But He did require Augustine to stop placing his confidence in his mind to distinguish truth from falsehood. The mind comes along later to help us interpret what our heart already knows.

Augustine began to trust a wholly different source of power for living, one that locates itself in the heart, not the mind. He began to realize that the Holy Spirit is the real power of God, who uses the Bible to infect hearts with the Truth of Jesus.

Third, the power of God does not answer to clever thinking or teaching, but to simple prayer, the prayer of faith. Augustine recognized that he had found peace not because of his brilliant thinking, but because his mother, Monica, had prayed "with pitiful and most sorrowful groanings."

Those who recognize God's power will spend the rest of their lives learning to pray. Out of prayer, they will hear God tell them whatever else He may desire of them. It is prayer, not human effort, that moves the hand and heart of God. Prayer is "the one thing needful." It is the life of prayer more than anything else that identifies what power we really believe in. "Windows" people will pray. "DOS" people will not.

■ ■ ■

Chapter Twenty-four

THE NEW AGE OPTION

Western thought has not remained static, but has moved on from where it was a century or even fifty years ago. A third world-view option has emerged, because large numbers of people have discovered another power source to live by: the spirit guides, the angels. Call them what you will, they are out there, and many people have discovered them as a source of knowledge and power. Inevitably, some have built their world-view around that power.

Carl Jung Discovers Mid-level Spirits

This third option began to emerge when the older DOS system was in full flower throughout Europe. It happened quietly, and few people were aware of it. Most people in the West thought that there was no such thing as spirit guides or angels or demons. They considered all such things superstition. But some few did believe in them, including a Swiss psychiatrist named Carl Jung.

Jung grew up in the home of his father ("a poor country parson" of Swiss Reformed persuasion) and mother. Of his mother he wrote that she "was somehow rooted in deep, invisible ground, though it never appeared to me as confidence in her Christian faith. For me it was somehow connected with animals, trees, mountains, meadows, and running water, all of which contrasted most strangely with her Christian surface and her conventional assertions of faith. ...It never occurred to me how "pagan" this foundation was."[1]

During his early years, Jung was struggling to discover a world-view that he could live with. He was not satisfied with the world-view that emerged from his poor country-parson father, but was much more influenced by his mother, and his grandfather, who was Grandmaster of the Swiss lodge of Freemasons. There were forces at work in Europe that fascinated Jung, and he was determined to explore them.

This exploration put him at odds with his mentor, Sigmund Freud. In his autobiography, *Memories, Dreams, Reflections*, Jung told of one particular encounter with Freud during a visit in 1909. Jung asked his mentor what he thought about parapsychology. Freud replied that he thought it was all bosh.

Jung felt that Freud was revealing a prejudice against the spiritual realm, and was about to make a sharp retort when suddenly, he had a curious sensation of heat in his diaphragm. Simultaneously, there came a loud bang from the bookcase nearby, and both men started up in alarm, thinking that the bookcase was about to topple over. Jung pointed out that this was a spiritual phenomenon of some sort. He called it a "catalytic exteriorization phenomenon."

"Oh come," Freud retorted. "That is sheer bosh."

"It is not," he replied. "You are mistaken, Herr Professor. And to prove my point I now predict that in a moment there will be another such loud report!" Sure enough, no sooner had he said those words than the same detonation went off in the bookcase.

Jung concludes: "Freud only stared aghast at me. ...This incident aroused his mistrust of me, and I had the feeling that I had done something against him"[2]

Jung accepted the reality of the spirit world. Freud, ensconced in his DOS world-view, did not.

A Third World-view, a Third Power Source

Jung went on to have a great many more experiences of the spirit realm during World War One. Several "daemonic" spirits became familiar to him. Often they went by biblical names (Elijah, Salome, Philemon, etc.).

He had categorically rejected the possibility that there could be evil motivations among these spirits, or that there could be deception in the world. So he set himself to learn from the beings he had discovered, despite the fact that some of these experiences were truly frightening. For instance, on one such night...

> *it began with a restlessness, but I did not know what it meant or what "they" wanted of me. There was an ominous atmosphere all around me. I had the strange feeling that the air was filled with ghostly entities. Then it was as if my house began to be haunted. My eldest daughter saw a white figure passing through the room. My second daughter, independently of her elder sister, related that twice in the night her blanket had been snatched away; and that same night my nine-year-old son had an anxiety dream.*[3]

In spite of these frightening experiences, Jung discovered that the beings in his house could be quite friendly, really, and that they were intelligent beings who bore listening to. Reflecting on what he learned from those encounters, he concludes:

> *Today I can say that I have never lost touch with my initial experiences. All my works, all my creative activity, has come from those initial fantasies and dreams which began in 1912, almost fifty years ago. Everything that I accomplished in later life was already contained in them....*[4]

Jung went on to be the foremost guru of the New Age movement, and to open the way for the demise of the DOS operating system represented by Freud. In the 1920's, he explored Gnosticism, and with the discovery of the original writings of the Gnostics of the second century at Nag Hammadi in the late '40s, it was Jung who popularized them, along with many other occult teachings, such as alchemy and Freemasonry.

Jung believed that everyone should be a part of an occult society, writing, "There is no better means of intensifying the treasured feeling of individuality than the possession of a secret which the individual is pledged to guard. The very beginnings of societal structures reveal the craving for secret organizations. When no valid secrets really exist, mysteries are invented or contrived to which privileged initiates are admitted. Such was the case with the Rosicrucians and many other societies."[5]

What Jung was offering to the world is an operating system that trusts a third power source—not God, not the rational mind, but mid-level spirits. Whole cultures and religions have grown up around this power source. Jung rediscovered it for the West in the first half of the last century, and, in the second half reintroduced it to the Western world.

Backtracking and Regression

Look at what was happening. Augustine had started with a New Age world-view and discarded it. Then he had tried the Enlightenment, and discarded it. Finally, he ended up at the power of God and convinced others to follow him. They followed him—and followed Christ—for 1,500 years.

Ironic, isn't it? Western thought seems to be crawling backwards through Augustine's pilgrimage, moving from where he ended up, back to the place where he started.

Jung, in researching alchemy, Gnosticism, Rosicrucianism and dozens of occult societies, was completely convinced that his rediscoveries of occultism would lead to a more complete and satisfying world-view than Freud's narrow and limited one. Like many who operate out of this world-view, he had no objection to Christianity and was willing to incorporate it into his system. "Not only do I leave the door open for the Christian message, but I consider it of central importance for Western man."[6] He believed that all the spiritual options are equally good and that there is no evil in the world.

The Sting

In retrospect, though, it was not his golden optimism that has proven true to reality, but the warnings of William James. If Freud was naïve about the existence of spirits, Jung was naïve about their evil intentions and the subtlety of their deception. ("Nature...harbors no intention to deceive," he wrote."[7])

During the 1940's, Jung recognized that Hitler's National Socialism grew out of the same world-view that he himself was developing—that Hitler gained his power from spirits, from "daemons." But the sheer evil of what was revealed by the end of World War Two caught Jung off guard.[8]

At the height of Europe's fascination with science, mid-level spirits were gaining entry to the lives of two key figures. The first was Kaiser Wilhelm, and the second was Adolf Hitler. In an earlier book, I have shown that both Kaiser Wilhelm and Hitler were members of occult societies, and had amassed whole libraries of occult books.[9] Their power and their ideas did indeed come from demons, and their closest friends understood this. Like Jung, they surrendered their lives to the power of middle-level spirits— not to the power of God.

But both of these men lived during a time when most Westerners, including Christians, did not believe in such things. They believed neither in the power of spirits, nor in the power of God. They had opted for the power of the rational mind—what we are calling the DOS system.

Rees Howells Intercedes

God, however, had not abandoned Europe. In answer to prayer, he poured out His Spirit in the great Welsh Revival of 1905. That Revival was itself the result of much prayer. Later He raised up an intercessor named Rees Howells. Howells was aware of the demonic power behind Hitler because the Holy Spirit revealed this to him. Jesus Christ raised up Rees Howells to oppose the power behind Nazism. The story of that prayer battle is found in the book, *Rees Howells, Intercessor*. This book shows convincingly that it is intercessors, laying hold of the means God has provided for His Church, who truly shape history.

The power of God trumps all other power. That is why we must return to our roots and believe in God's power again.

■ ■ ■

Chapter Twenty-five

CHOOSING GOD AGAIN

The last significant season of awakening among us occurred in 1905. Significant prayer for that outpouring of power began in 1900. When R. A. Torrey became president of the Chicago Bible Institute (renamed the Moody Bible Institute after the death of D. L. Moody in 1899), Torrey heard God say that he must organize prayer for a massive worldwide awakening. In the first month of the new century he began weekly prayer meetings to that end. Two years later, God instructed Torrey to embark on an evangelistic tour of Australia, and Torrey's career as a world-renowned evangelist began in 1903. Torrey's presence was a significant factor in the awakening of 1904 known as the Welsh Revival.

Torrey's friend, the Canadian Presbyterian Jonathan Goforth, presided over awakenings in Korea and China.

The Presbyterian, John Hyde, graduate of McCormick Theological Seminary, known as "Praying Hyde," presided over awakenings in north India.[1] In those days, there was a remnant of Americans who, like William James, still believed in the power of God to awaken whole nations.

Jonathan Goforth

However, when these men returned to home base after seasons of extraordinary ministry, they ran into serious conflict with Western Christians to whom they tried to convey their excitement. Jonathan Goforth wrote two books, *When the Spirit's Fire Swept Korea* and *By My Spirit* about his work in China. These books are full of the accounts of God's wonders. They make for exciting reading.

But Goforth did not find that his Canadian Christian audience appreciated his experiences at all:

> *The ministerial association of a certain city in the homeland once invited me to tell them about the Spirit's quickening work in China. In my address I assured them that I had no reason to consider myself any special favorite of the Almighty. What God had done through me in China I was sure He was able and willing to do through them in Canada. Hence that every minister should have the faith and courage to look to God the Holy Spirit to revive His people. I went on to point out that John Wesley and his colleagues were just ordinary men until their hearts were touched by the Divine fire. At that*

*point a Methodist preacher of some note
interrupted me. "What, sir!" he exclaimed; "do
you mean to tell me that we don't preach better
now than John Wesley ever did?" "Are you
getting John Wesley's results?" I asked.*

*On another occasion I was asked to address a
meeting of the Presbyterian Synod in Toronto. I
took as my theme the revival at Changtehfu in
1908. I look back to that revival as perhaps the
mightiest of the Spirit that I have ever been
through. During those wonderful ten days there
were seven different times that I was prevented
from giving an address owing to the great
brokenness among the people. While I was
addressing the Synod, a certain theological
professor, sitting at a table nearby, looked
anything but happy. My account of the Holy
Spirit's convicting power over a Chinese audience
seemed to put his nerves all on edge. I understand
that there was another professor from the same
seminary who was sitting in another part of the
building, and that he, too, fidgeted in his seat
most uneasily. It seems that he finally turned
around and hissed—"Rats!" ...Can we wonder
that spirituality is at so low an ebb throughout
Christendom? Thirty-two percent of the
Protestant churches in the United States report no
increasing in membership in 1927.²*

R. A. Torrey

For his part, R. A. Torrey returned to California to be embroiled in controversy.

Dr. Torrey was unable to convey his message in the midst of an increasingly volatile and controversial atmosphere. In the years before his death in 1928, he formed the World's Christian Fundamentals Association. He wanted to get Christian teaching down to its basic elements in order to present the Gospel to the world more effectively and make disciples in every nation. Unfortunately he lived to see fundamentalism become a narrow, sniping, dogmatizing influence in America, devoid of the power of the Holy Spirit to win an increasingly skeptical, doubting world to Christ.

...Fundamentalism would concentrate not on fulfilling the basics of faith and power to complete the Great Commission, but on gaining political control over seminaries and denominations against the perceived danger of liberalism. Evangelicals, for their part, could not see that it is by the power of God, not political control, that the soul of the Church stays healthy.[3]

Is Science the Enemy?

Then, of course, the Scopes trial came down the pike. This tragic event twisted the truth so that the issue became "God *versus* science." This, of course, was never the issue, and it still isn't.

When Descartes, a Christian, first wrote his "Method of Rightly Conducting the Reason," which established Enlightenment thinking, Blaise Pascal objected: "I cannot forgive Descartes. In all his philosophy he would have been quite willing to dispense with God. But he could not help granting him a flick of the forefinger to start the world in motion; beyond this, he has no further need of God."[4] Pascal was not opposed to science. He himself had written several scientific treatises. Pascal was opposed to the DOS worldview that abandoned the power of God at the heart of both the natural and spiritual realms.

The World-view Does the Filtering

Once you have bought into that world-view, as Americans did 80 or 90 years ago, the world-view itself begins to filter your view of things. World-views open our eyes to certain aspects of our world, but blind us from seeing others. This all happens at a subconscious level. We are not even aware of this. Our world-view lies underneath our eyesight filtering everything automatically, helping us to digest an impossibly complex world to simplify it so that our meager brains can handle the data.

When you believe in the power of the rational mind working on the natural world to control it, you will see only that which supports your world-view. Miracles? Awakened hearts? Converted people? Answers to prayer? These things are treated as unimportant anomalies. Your mind discards such things as quickly as possible, to move on to what it considers important.

It is possible that professors of the last century did not intend to leave out the Great Awakenings of our past from the story of our history. I believe that their world-view did this subconsciously. Once they had installed the DOS world-view as their personal operating system, the world-view did the rest, filtering out data about spiritual power that did not fit the prevailing culture.

The Knife-edge of Decision

Today, however, the scene has changed. No world-view prevails among us. Americans believe a mish-mash of this and that. Some are New-agers. Some are hard-core DOS believers. Some are true believers in what we have called Windows. They believe that the world still has God at the heart of it as described in the Bible.

Let me close this section with a quote from my friend, Tom White. Tom serves the city-wide church where I started ministry 35 years ago, in Corvallis, Oregon. Tom's recent book, *City-wide Prayer Movements* is a must for those who long for the manifestation of God's power and presence among us.

> *In a season of spiritual darkness, we always find a remnant that embraces repentance and cries out to the Lord for a return of his favor. Such cries, heard in recent years across the landscape of nations and cities, sound like the sons of Korah, a desperate plea and a probing question: "Restore us again, O God our Savior,*

and put away your displeasure toward us...
Will you not revive us again, that your people
may rejoice in you?" (Psalms 85:4,6)

What gets our God's attention are humble
hearts breaking over sin, yearning for his
nearness, and persevering to pray until his glory
dwells "in our land." Do we honestly have more
than a half-hearted desire for some measure of
spiritual refreshment? Or are we so intoxicated
by earthly culture that we cannot even discern the
departure of divine glory?[5]

■ ■ ■

Chapter Twenty-six

GOD'S GLORY FOR A NATION

Many people have had difficulty discerning the departure of God's glory from our country. Often, this has happened when a spirit of domination and control has taken over the Christian Church, and the Church itself has become corrupt.

At that point, the man on the street lost his bearings, and could not discern God at all. He actually associated the name of Jesus with the hurt he experienced from Christians, and his picture of God became tainted. No one was modeling out the love and humility of Christ.

In this way, whole nations have become trapped in deception, unable to see God or believe in His goodness. At such times, there is a loss of confidence in the power of God, and large numbers of people turn to the rational mind as their only hope. The DOS world-view takes over and prevails against a biblical world-view. But the DOS world-view is a dead-end road.

The French Track Record

I have shown that Thomas Jefferson was among the first to advance this world-view in this country. He gained his ideas from France, where this world-view originated for Europeans. Because this world-view has a track record two centuries long by now, we can see what has resulted from it in France. History is ultimately the track record of ideas. To see whether the ideas are valid or not, we have only to look at the history of those countries that tried the ideas. In this case, that country is France.

The French passed through a season in the 18th century when the Church was taken over by a spirit of domination and control. The Catholic Church during the Renaissance years showed much evidence of that spirit, the spirit of the Inquisition. At that period, the Roman Catholic Church was so corrupt that there were three popes at once vying for power. One of these had his power base at Avignon in France. At that time, too, the Catholic Church maintained that slavery was ordained of God and gave its official stamp of approval to the African slave trade. Under then-current teaching, Catholics like Christopher Columbus took slaves in the West Indies, believing that slavery is a good way of "saving" Indians. This is the gospel according to the spirit of domination and control.

The French Revolution

The French responded to the bad witness of the (royalist) French Catholic Church by rejecting Christ, confiscating church properties to finance the revolution, and by turning to Rene Descartes, Voltaire and Rousseau as their guides. These leaders rejected not only the negative aspects of Christian leadership—those that had sent the Huguenots migrating to this country. They also rejected their own great Christian thinkers going back to Irenaeus, John Calvin, Francois Fenelon, Mme. Guyon, Jean-Pierre de Caussade, Blaise Pascal and a host of others. In a single generation, the French un-converted themselves, moving from Christianity to deism to full-fledged atheism. Today, fewer than 1% of French people are Christians.

The Hope of the Rational Mind

In contrast to the American Revolution, the French Revolution was an anti-God movement, a national experiment with the DOS world-view that closed out the spirit world entirely. DOS would be their pathway to *la gloire de la France*, a nation freed from all superstitious faith, to pursue "real" knowledge. This, of course, was the vision of Descartes. But, as we have seen, the ideas of the revolution, so pristine in theory, produced the power of the guillotine, a very irrational instrument of terrorism. After that, Napoleon promised to extend his own version of domination over the whole earth, using Paris as his capital.

Undaunted by these monumental disasters, during the 1850's and '60's, the French turned to their universities to extend learning, in order to take control of the world through the sheer power of education. French science and engineering became the hope of France, and that hope culminated in the leadership of two great engineers. It was in engineering, after all, that scientific theories would be tested in gaining actual mastery over the world. The first of these engineers, Alexandre Gustave Eiffel, in 1889 built a great tower in Paris reaching to the heavens. The other, Ferdinand de Lesseps, built a great canal to connect the Mediterranean with the Gulf of Suez.

La Gloire de la France

Encouraged by these two great triumphs of the Enlightenment, Ferdinand de Lesseps proposed to his countrymen the *piéce de resistance*—a canal that would connect the Atlantic with the Pacific Oceans at the Isthmus of Panama. The idea was partly inspired by Jules Verne's novel, *Around the World in Eighty Days*, published in 1872.

A team was gathered together to build the canal. Though it was to be an international team, the French conspired to control the project from start to finish. They wanted to bring glory to France, and to the new principles of science and the rational mind that they now believed with all their hearts.

From the beginning, problems were encountered, then more problems, and more still. As the years passed, workers were dying like flies from malaria, and each problem with the Panamanian terrain cost more money, and more still.

When the money ran out, De Lesseps, a man of great persuasive ability, convinced large numbers of French people to contribute their life savings to this project—for, he said, the glory of France was at stake. He was brimming with self-assurance, saying: "I maintain that (the canal at) Panama will be easier to make, easier to complete, and easier to keep up than Suez."[1] The French believed in him because they believed in themselves. They believed in their nation and the education that would prevail over the older ideas they had superseded.

In the end, the great engineer bled France dry, and then admitted defeat on Feb. 4, 1889. The people of France, bitterly disillusioned, turned against de Lesseps, and filled his latter days with lawsuits. The huge machines invented by French engineers were left to rust in the perpetual rains of Panama.

This was a financial and political disaster for France. The nation never recovered from it. The story that follows is the story of a weak and disillusioned nation tossed about by other powers greater than itself. The French were soon to be tormented and humiliated by forces of great darkness. Powers were gathering in Germany which broke out in war. France has never recovered from the disasters of the 18th and 19th centuries and the two great wars that followed. By no stretch of the imagination can these experiments in godless science be considered a success.

Those who have studied the story of the Panama Canal, so well told by David McCullough in *The Path Between the Seas*, will know that it was science and medicine that finally conquered the dreaded malaria that decimated the teams of canal builders. But godless science is a very different thing from a science based on the loving and overarching purposes of God. Descartes represents one way of thinking. Pascal another. Americans, who did manage to complete the project some twenty years later, made many mistakes, too. Our Canal project was not entirely guided by noble motives. Still, the story of the sacrificial love of scientists who were willing to lay down their lives (literally lying in beds of filth to prove that it was not filth but mosquitoes that caused malaria) is an inspiration of humility and compassionate love at work through scientific inquiry.

Some would say, "Well, the French should not be faulted for trying great things. They just had a run of bad luck."

Those who begin with a DOS world-view will resort to "bad luck" whenever their world-view does not yield the results they thought it would. Those of us with a Windows world-view, when we look at French history, might well conclude, "This is just what you would expect in a nation that has rejected the power of God."

Today, Jesus is still calling to the French people to return to Him. In the year 2000, a French Christian, Jackie Minard, came to Richmond representing the Christians of France. He came to plead for prayer that God might grant a spiritual awakening in his country.

Awakening in South Africa

Let's look elsewhere now for a more encouraging story—to the nation of South Africa, where we began in Chapter One. Here, God has raised up Christian leaders— "prophets, priests and kings"—to provide His kind of courageous leadership to lead their country out from under the clouds of domination and control and into the light of spiritual awakening. This leadership helped South Africa repudiate its history of apartheid, and to prevent a French-Revolution-style bloodbath after the fall of that system.

Let me share the better part of a recent interview with a friend, Paul Vorster, who moved from Johannesburg to Richmond recently. He described the progressive emergence of his country from spiritual darkness to light.

When I was a kid, the black churches were crying out for the unrighteousness, for the injustices. It was a cry of pain from the horrible things that were happening to them. It was a prayer movement driven by a lot of pain.

On the other side, the white people justified their actions through the word of God. A lot of things were taken way out of control, but at the start they were close to God. Those Dutch who first came here during the years of British rule saw themselves as Voortrekkers—they saw themselves as Hebrews moving from a land of bondage to a land of freedom. They were tremendously devoted to prayer. They prayed before every battle they won.

But as the years passed, fear took control because they were a tiny minority. Blacks were seen as animals, they weren't even seen as people. There were others like Andrew Murray, men of prayer. I believe they were praying for the fall of apartheid, whether they knew it or not.

Let me break in here to explain what most people know, that South Africa developed an increasingly repressive system, called apartheid, by which a tiny minority of Dutch people ruled a vast majority of blacks. But then in the early '90's, through the leadership of F. W. de Klerk, South Africa broke away from apartheid by holding free elections. De Klerk provides us with a good illustration of the "kingly" or governing office under Christ as he related to the "prophetic" position of Archbishop Desmond Tutu.

De Klerk, as much as any Church leader, gained his primary identity in Christ. Russ Parker, in his excellent book, *Healing Wounded History*, describes an interview with de Klerk at Royal Albert Hall after the fall of apartheid:

He was asked whether it was international sanctions which had brought about the end of apartheid. De Klerk replied, "It was not the sanctions, but a deep self-analysis on our knees before God."[2]

Now I want to show how the obedience of political leaders to overthrow the spirit of domination and control cleared the way for a time of refreshing from the presence of the Lord. I continue my interview with Paul Vorster, who reflects on his personal experience of the Holy Spirit:

The day the elections first took place, many groups were fighting amongst each other. It wasn't just between black and white. Many were threatening to start a war. It would have been a war that no police system could have maintained, there were too many people who were mad, and ready to go into action.

There was so much fear, but for some it was a day of great joy. As a result of the elections, the African National Congress came into power. A lot of the A.N.C. leaders had been educated by white missionaries.

In those early days, they were thinking about war tribunals to put people on trial for what they had done under apartheid. But the new leaders recognized that they needed some kind of different answer, so they started the Truth and Reconciliation Commission. Desmond Tutu was one of the Christians on this committee. Everyone criticized the Truth and Reconciliation Commission when it started. But the Commission gave people the opportunity to confess what they had done, and they would be given amnesty. The police commissioners would go on trial and tell the truth of what they did and why they did it. Some of the people had no regret for what they had done. Others would break down in deep repentance.

On the other side, victims would give testimony of what had happened to them. There were people who had lost children; horrible things had happened. The Commission would hear both sides of the story. They were able to communicate across the chasm of apartheid, and that began to heal the country. There is no transformation without truthfulness. We have to be able to look at things exactly for what they were. Only then can we really experience transformation.

Political things and spiritual things are not really that separated. Political changes and spiritual change are intertwined. With the fall of apartheid, the spiritual climate began to change.

The move of God beginning in the late '90's was so great all over Johannesburg—it was among all people and all colors and all ages. God was so in control of it, the Church I attended went from 25,000 members to 35,000 members in a year. They had 900 small groups. It was amazing to see that.

Everything immediately changed in my life. Not just for me, but for all my friends. We would gather together to drink coffee. It was a big coffee culture. And that's when God would show up and that's when God manifested, not in church but

*when we would get together for coffee.
I mean, I didn't set foot in church until a year
later. We would get together just praying together,
and then God would send people in our path. It
wasn't pastor so-and-so having a crusade or some
outreach. It was just God showing up in circles of
people.*

*Let me go back to the beginning to tell my
own personal story. I worked in a neighborhood
in Johannesburg that was known as a gangster
neighborhood. One day, I was sitting in my car
with my window open. I saw this kid walking past
my car. I thought he was about 14 years old, and
I could tell he wasn't a gangster. When he was in
the middle of the road, he stopped and turned
and pointed his finger at me just out of the blue.
He said to me in my own language, Afrikaans,
"You'd better smile because God loves you."*

*For the first time in my life, I experienced the
presence of God, right there. I just had the sense
that God was with me and that things would be
okay. Nine months later, I went on a drinking
holiday to Cape Town with some of my drinking
friends. While in Cape Town, I happened to meet
a girl who was from Johannesburg. I knew that
something was different about her. At the time,
she was taking a Bible class at her church, so for
the next three months, I would drop her off at her
church. After three months, I knew I needed
something she had. She prayed for me to be*

Spirit-filled. It was very casual, just talking about stuff. But God instantly set me free from alcohol, smoking, a lot of things I was into. Very radical. A lot of my friends were drug addicts. They were also changed just like me.

God would just meet people out in worldly places. That's how it had been for this girl, the girl that prayed for me. She had been the daughter of a well-known minister. She was drinking with her friends in a pub. Suddenly she felt that God wanted her to get up and leave the building. As she walked out the door, she got Spirit-filled. She sobered up immediately. Back in the pub all her friends were partying. She immediately went back and told all her friends about Jesus. That's how she got Spirit-filled. Just an answer to prayer. Nobody "evangelized" her.

The Kingdom of God was manifesting. Everything was changing. There's a sense of God's being there. It's unexplainable. The only thing you want to think about or talk about is Jesus. God is there all the time. It doesn't matter what's going on. You just know that God is there. And it's intense. The atmosphere is intense. I don't want to super-spiritualize everything. But really, you cannot help but notice there is something in the air.

Then sometimes there would be resistance, a spiritual resistance. It would be brief, like a couple of days. It would be extremely dark. You'd just continue in prayer for a little while. And God would break in, and all those things would flee.

Because I've seen Revival, I've seen what God can do, I know I will pray for Revival for the rest of my life. And it's just because when you've seen it, you know what it is. It's kind of unnatural for a young guy like me to want to pray for these things. But it grips you so much.

In South Africa, there's still a lot of violence, and the root of apartheid is still working itself out. But sin is seen for what it is there. People are blatant about their sins. When they repent, they are blatant about their repentance. Here it's very different, it's more blended. I'll be honest with you. I'm unsatisfied here in Richmond. But it's a godly dissatisfaction. I know there is more for Richmond, because I've seen it in South Africa. [3]

God has been leading many people like Paul to Richmond, people moving here from all over the world who have experienced spiritual transformation elsewhere. For those of us who have grown up in the West, some of our most basic assumptions about life will be challenged during the coming years. Will we be ready?

Our readiness surely must be measured by our surrender to Christ, so that we can become vessels of leadership He can use to bring transformation to our city, and to our country.

Let me close with this wonderful summation from Rhonda Hughey, who works with George Otis, Jr. in shepherding city-wide transformation around the world:

> *The critical component to revival in the church and transformation in the community is the manifest presence of Jesus. In transformed communities, the presence of God is a valued and critical component of the well-being of the community at every level of society. Participants in transformation in these communities include presidents, prime ministers, mayors, businessmen, law enforcement officers, clergy, and laypeople. People from all over the world are gathering to cry out to God and labor together to seek His presence and the transformation of their communities.*

> *We must become hungry and thirsty for more of Jesus in our midst. We must cry out in desperation for God's presence to be restored in our lives, our churches, and ultimately in our cities. We must treasure the manifest presence of God, because as Jesus said in John 15:5, "Without Me you can do nothing."* [4]

■ ■ ■

AFTERWORD

My aim in this book has been to lay foundations for a spiritual awakening. In our hurry to get God's work done, we Western Christians tend to build shallow foundations, then we try to build skyscrapers on top of them. I believe that God has been helping many Richmonders build deep foundations so that we can build a stronger structure on top of them. These, then, are the foundational principles I have introduced:

Surrender.
Reliance on God's power.
Humility and love.

We need these strong foundations before we build. But then we also need to build. In these last few pages let me recommend some resources for builders.

God is putting together leaders right now who can build a city "whose architect and builder is God" (Heb. 11:10). The following recommendations are given in hopes of getting these leaders on the same page as we move toward the transformation of a city. Those who sense that God is speaking to them about Richmond as a gateway of spiritual awakening should begin equipping ourselves with the instructions to build according to the principles and methods of God's Kingdom. These are very different from humanly devised principles and methods. The following videos and books give sound guidance based on what God is doing elsewhere around the world.

First, I refer you to George Otis, Jr.'s *Quickenings* video, available at SentinelGroup.org. From his vast experience with hundreds of communities worldwide, George cites seven principles of city-wide transformation, articulated by the people in those communities. I list these seven points briefly, just to entice you to buy the video:

1) God wants to be invited into our communities.

2) God is drawn to holiness and humility.

3) Corporate Revival begins with individual obedience.

4) Biblical unity among a small minority commands the blessing of God.

5) Breakthrough prayer releases God's destiny for a community.

6) God's work will always be unique to a community. (God cannot be predicted or stage managed.)

7) God uses servant leaders who persevere.

The *Quickenings* video also describes the most common barriers and hindrances to transformation. The video is an absolute must for those who wish to lead Richmond into city-wide transformation. We simply must understand what God is doing world-wide if we are to break free from the wrong assumptions and outdated wineskins to which we Americans cling.

Second, I recommend Rhonda Hughey's book, *Desperate for His Presence*, available from Fusionministry.com. Rhonda "fuses" the ministry of George Otis, Jr. (pursuing city-wide transformation) with the ministry of the International House of Prayer in Kansas City (pursuing intimacy with God). Rhonda calls us to pray for a greater hunger for God, without which there cannot be spiritual awakening. As long as we don't really believe that we need God, He will not come to bestow His presence in Richmond. In addition, Rhonda lists the following transitions in the Church that must happen if a city is to be transformed:

1) From suspicion to trust,

2) From functional unity to relational unity,

3) From horizontal agreement to vertical agreement,

4) From Revival visitation to transforming habitation,

5) From empire building to kingdom building,

6) From workers to lovers,

7) From warriors to worshipers,

8) From "sacred vs. secular" to Kingdom focused,

9) From the methods of man to the presence of God,

Again, I simply list these in hopes that you will buy the book. Rhonda, who has visited Richmond twice, feels a particular calling to maintain a relationship with us for the long haul. She said during a recent visit that she senses that Richmond has made great advancements in building the foundations toward transformation.

A third book I highly recommend is *Healing Wounded History,* by Russ Parker. Russ brings a wealth of experience and a confluence of lessons from around the world, especially from countries struggling out of deep wounds of the past—Ireland, England, South Africa and Rwanda. He stresses that personal healing cannot touch unhealed community wounds which often run deeper than personal wounds. These are wounds that a whole people group has suffered at the hands of another people group. God can heal group wounds. Russ conveys the biblical principles for this healing of groups with wounded history. At the heart of his book, he lists the dynamics of reconciliation:

1) Remembering trauma, allowing stories to be told and heard

2) Lamenting the trauma together

3) Confessing the sins of the group (perhaps by

representatives of the group who may not have been personally involved)

4) Repentance: developing a life style "in the opposite spirit"

Russ articulates well the biblical roots of these healing principles.

A fourth resource is Ruth Ruibal's book, *Unity in the Spirit*, available from Sentinelgroup.org. Ruth, the wife of slain leader Julio Ruibal of Cali, Colombia, is featured in the *Transformations* video mentioned in Chapter One of this book. Ruth traces the struggle for Church unity in Cali, so important in obtaining the manifest presence of God in that city. Again, the principles she describes come out of vast experience with proven results. Unity is far easier to talk about than to achieve! Ruth conveys the difficulties we are likely to experience in the pursuit of Christian unity, and how to overcome them.

A fifth resource is Tom White's book, *City-wide Prayer Movements*. Like the others recommended above, Tom has gained his perspective from many countries around the world that are at the front edge of God's redemptive movements in cities. Tom understands that nothing of God's kingdom is birthed without unified, significant prayer, and he has provided significant leadership in many of the cities of the world—Tokyo, St. Petersburg, Jerusalem, New Delhi and cities of the United States. He is well acquainted with the minefields through which Christians must struggle to attain unity and invite the manifest presence of God.

By gaining from the experience of others who have already walked through these minefields, we may avoid crippling explosions here in Richmond. Leaders: let's equip ourselves the best we can. We must get ready for what God will do, drawing together with singleness of purpose, surrendered lives, and a humble, loving pursuit of Jesus.

■ ■ ■

END NOTES

Chapter One

1 Taken from *www.transformationafrica.org/t_testimony.html*.

2 Mark Noll, Sprunt Lectures, Union Theological Seminary, January 24, 2005.

Chapter Two

1 Alfred Edersheim, *The Life and Times of Jesus the Messiah* (Grand Rapids: Eerdmans, 1971).

Chapter Three

1 Iain H. Murray, *The Puritan Hope* (Edinburgh: Banner of Truth, 1971), p. 5, quoting John Knox, *History of the Reformation in Scotland*, Vol. 1.

2 Murray, p. 5.

3 Murray, p. 5.

4 Murray, p. 5, from a letter dated June 23, 1559.

Chapter Four

1 Letter from John Wesley to William Wilberforce, Feb. 24, 1791.

2 From Hugh Thomas, *The Slave Trade* (New York: Simon and Schuster, 1997), pp. 156.

3 James Walvin, *Black Ivory* (Oxford: Blackwell, 2001), p. 30.

4 John Newton, "Thoughts on the African Slave Trade" Letters and Sermons (Edinburgh, 1780), p. 103.

Chapter Five

1 Jonathan Goforth, *By My Spirit, Classic Books for Today* (Newton, Kansas: Herald of His Coming), p. 1.

2 Goforth, p. 1.

3 William Lee Miller, *Arguing About Slavery* (New York: Knopf, 1997), pp. 80-81.

4 Peter Marshall and David Manuel, *Sounding Forth the Trumpet* (Grand Rapids: Revell, 1997), p. 80.

5 Harvey Cox, *Fire from Heaven* (Reading, Massachusetts: Addison-Wesley, 1995), p. 58.

Chapter Six

1 Mark Noll: Sprunt Lectures, January 24, 2005.

2 William Bradford, *Of Plimouth Plantation 1620-1647* (New York: Random House, 1981), pp. 23-26.

3 Virginius Dabney, *Richmond: The Story of a City* (Charlottesville: University Press of Virginia, 1990), p. 5.

4 John Winthrop, "Portrait of a Covenant Community," reprint by Charles Crismier, Save America Ministries, p. 1.

5 Robert Bluford, Jr., *Living on the Borders of Eternity* (Mechanicsville, Virginia: Historic Polegreen Foundation, 2004), pp. 22-23.

6 Harry M. Ward, *Richmond: An Illustrated History* (Northridge, California: Windsor, 1985), p. 8.

7 Dabney, p. 11.

8 "First Virginia Charter," April 10, 1606.

Chapter Seven

1 Bluford, p. 21.

2 Murray, p. 73.

3 Murray, pp. 73-74.

4 Fawn M. Brodie, *Thomas Jefferson: An Intimate History* (New York: Bantam, 1974), p. 50.

5 Brodie, p. 51.

6 Brodie, p. 232. From a letter to Jean Nicolas Demeunier, June 26, 1786.

Chapter Eight

1 Irving Stone, *Those Who Love, A Biographical Novel of Abigail and John Adams* (New York: Doubleday, 1965), p. 125. From "Response to William Pym."

2 Miller, p. 157.

3 Both quotes are from Miller, p. 162.

4 Miller, p. 159.

5 Miller, p. 185.

6 Dabney, p. 60.

7 Ward, pp. 94-95.

8 Ward, p. 105.

9 Miller, p. 11.

10 Ward, p. 107.

11 Ward, p. 107.

Chapter Nine

1 Dabney, p. 162.

2 Louis Albert Banks, *Religious Life of Famous Americans* (Boston: American Tract Society, 1904), pp. 7-8.

3 Banks, p. 5.

4 Dabney, p. 195.

5 Dabney, pp. 197-198.

6 "Richmond: The Book" Richmond, the Complete Sourcebook: 2005 edition, p. 25.

Chapter Ten

1 Ward, p. 155.

2 Interview with Dr. Robert Taylor, at his home, June, 2004.

3 Peter Hardin, "Documentary Genocide," *Richmond Times-Dispatch*, March 5, 2000, p. A-1.

Chapter Eleven

1 Dabney, p. 206.

Chapter Twelve

1 Mike Bickle, *Growing in the Prophetic* (Lake Mary, Florida: Creation House, 1996), pp. 44-45.

2 Martin Luther, "Exposition on John 14:12."

Chapter Seventeen

1 Address by Mark Anderson, International House of Prayer, Kansas City, August 21, 2004.

Chapter Nineteen

1 Delores Winder and Bill Keith, *Jesus Set Me Free* (Shreveport, Louisiana: Fellowship Foundation, 1982), p. 4.

2 John Eidsmoe, *Christianity and the Constitution* (Grand Rapids: Baker, 1987), p. 41.

Chapter Twenty

1 Jonathan Edwards, *A Faithful Narrative of the Surprising Work of God* (Grand Rapids, Baker, 1979), pp. 16-17.

2 Jonathan Edwards, *The Life and Diary of David Brainerd* (Chicago: Moody, original date, 1758), pp. 143-145.

3 Charles G. Finney, *Memoirs* (Grand Rapids: Zondervan, 1989), p. 166-167.

Chapter Twenty-one

1 William James, *The Varieties of Religious Experience* (New York: International Free Press, 1948), p. 54-55.

2 James, p. 140.

3 James, p. 405.

Chapter Twenty-two

1 Sigmund Freud, *The Future of an Illusion* (New York: Liveright, 1928), pp. 95.

2 Freud, p. 68.

Chapter Twenty-three

1 Augustine, *Confessions*, VI.7.

2 Augustine, *Confessions*, VI. 6.

3 James, p. 74.

4 Augustine, *Confessions*, VI.7.

5 Augustine, *Confessions*, VI.3.

6 Augustine, *Confessions*, VIII.19.

7 Augustine, *Confessions*, VIII. 30.

Chapter Twenty-four

1 Carl G. Jung, *Memories, Dreams, Reflections* (New York: Vintage, 1963), p. 90.

2 Jung, pp. 155-156.

3 Jung, p. 190.

4 Jung, p. 192.

5 Jung, p. 342.

6 Jung, p. 210.

7 Jung, p. 161.

8 See Jeffrey Satinover's review of Richard C. Noll's book, *The Jung Cult* in "First Things," October, 1995, pp. 56-61.

9 Brad Long and Douglas McMurry, *The Collapse of the Brass Heaven*, (Grand Rapids: Chosen, 1994).

Chapter Twenty-five

1 See J. Edwin Orr, *Evangelical Awakenings in India*.

2 Goforth, p. 2.

3 Zeb Bradford Long and Douglas McMurry, *Receiving the Power* (Grand Rapids: Chosen, 1996), p. 49.

4 Blaise Pascal, Pensees, II.77.

5 Tom White, *City-wide Prayer Movements* (Ann Arbor: Servant, 2001), p. 159.

Chapter Twenty-six

1 David McCullough, *The Path Between the Seas* (New York: Touchstone, 1977), p. 101.

2 Russ Parker, *Healing Wounded History* (London: Darton, Longman and Todd, 2001), p. 59.

3 Personal interview with Paul Vorster, April, 2005.

4 Rhonda Hughey, *Desperate for His Presence* (Minneapolis: Bethany, 2004), p. 29.

■ ■ ■